MW01132567

ACCELERATED MANIFESTING

7 HIDDEN SECRETS

— TO —

SUPERCHARGE YOUR REALITY,
RAPIDLY SHIFT YOUR IDENTITY, AND SPEED UP
THE MANIFESTATION OF YOUR DESIRES

RYUU SHINOHARA

Omen
Publishing

© **Copyright Ryuu Shinohara 2021 - All rights reserved.**

The content contained within this book may not be reproduced, duplicated or transmitted without direct written permission from the author or the publisher.

Under no circumstances will any blame or legal responsibility be held against the publisher, or author, for any damages, reparation, or monetary loss due to the information contained within this book. Either directly or indirectly. You are responsible for your own choices, actions, and results.

Legal Notice:

This book is copyright protected. This book is only for personal use. You cannot amend, distribute, sell, use, quote or paraphrase any part, or the content within this book, without the consent of the author or publisher.

Disclaimer Notice:

Please note the information contained within this document is for educational and entertainment purposes only. All effort has been executed to present accurate, up to date, and reliable, complete information. No warranties of any kind are declared or implied. Readers acknowledge that the author is not engaged in the rendering of legal, financial, medical or professional advice.

The content within this book has been derived from various sources. Please consult a licensed professional before attempting any techniques outlined in this book.

By reading this document, the reader agrees that under no circumstances is the author responsible for any losses, direct or indirect, which are incurred as a result of the use of the information contained within this document, including, but not limited to, errors, omissions, or inaccuracies.

Interior formatting: Kozakura @ Fiverr

HOW TO GET THE MOST OUT OF THIS BOOK

I see it all the time. People read LOA book after LOA book without ever taking action on any of the insights they've gained or concepts they've learned. The last thing I want is for you to read this book, forget everything you read, and continue to live as you've lived. You picked this book up for a reason: to manifest positive change. These additional resources will help you along this journey.

>> Scan the QR Code to gain exclusive access
to these resources <<

Free Bonus #1: Manifestor Masterlist

In this document, you'll discover the top 3 daily habits for manifesting a life beyond your wildest dreams. Includes a simple layout to track your progress and instructions to get started today.

Free Bonus #2: Intention Journal

Journaling doesn't need to take 10 minutes away from your morning routine. In fact, if you structure it right, you can get it done in under a minute. This intention journal focuses on the essential components that make this practice so powerful.

Free Bonus #3: 4 Subtle Meditation Mistakes to Avoid

A deep meditative state can be challenging to come by. The mind and body will do everything possible to stop you from fully surrendering. If you truly want to maximize the benefits of your meditation practice, check out this document to avoid making the same mistakes millions are making.

Free Bonus #4: Meditation Design

There are many different ways to meditate. After testing many other methods, I've put together a step-by-step structure that I've found to be the most effective for deepening your state and embodying the future you.

Free Bonus #5: 4-Step Conscious Business Acceleration

Being an entrepreneur and business owner comes with many unique challenges and struggles. In this document, we'll tackle the top 3 blocks that are stopping most people from experiencing quantum leaps in their financial and business ventures.

Free Bonus #6: Vision Calendar

Are you struggling with consistency and clarity? The Vision Calendar is tailored to outline your daily/monthly/quarterly/yearly goals and intentions into bite-size pieces to prevent overwhelm and confusion.

Free Bonus #7: 4 Anti-Manifestation Practices

Sometimes people make mistakes. That's okay. Other times, they unconsciously sabotage themselves without even knowing it. This document will outline commonly taught manifestation practices that work against you and how to shift them to your benefit.

To get your free bonuses go to:

https://omenpublishing.activehosted.com/f/23

Or scan the QR Code below

TABLE OF CONTENTS

INTRODUCTION

In a world of instant gratification, waiting for your heart's desire to manifest can be painful. We're conditioned to 'get what we want now,' and when we're faced with delays or setbacks, we can question our beliefs. Sometimes, we can even conjure up old negative programming and engage in victimhood or self-loathing.

Fortunately, this isn't the case for you. Instead, you try to figure out how you can *speed up* your manifesting. You become proactive in your pursuit for a better life. You apply all the techniques, read all the books, and watch all the videos, yet there's no obvious shift in sight. Why are you still not getting results? There could be a myriad of reasons, but one thing is clear—there is a unique frustration that comes when you *believe* something will happen and it doesn't.

Many people have asked about this topic over the years. I've waited for an opportune time to explore these concepts in book form. The book you are holding in your hands is THAT book!

Most people have an erroneous idea about the Law of Attraction—they believe that by holding an intention, the world will accommodate your desires without you having to do anything. If you subscribe to this idea, you're not to blame. There are many teachers who promise riches, true love, and your ideal life through the ideals of 'wishful thinking.' Their teachings produce a temporary burst of manifestation motivation, but nothing else. They promote a message of 'easy manifesting' and while that can work for *lesser desires*—such as emergency manifestations—when you're working with your soul's purpose and your heart's *true* desires, there will be resistance in the form of overwhelm, confusion, indecisiveness, and many other reactions that manifest because of a shaky energetic foundation.

Intention is objective thinking combined with action. While it's nice to think we can simply desire something and reality will shift to accommodate it, it hardly ever works that way. After all, if wishful thinking were the answer to all your problems, you wouldn't be reading this book, would you? There are ways of optimizing your intentions so you accelerate the rate of positive changes you can experience. We need to introduce an additional element to the equation—and when we do, attaining what you want in life will seem effortless.

A POINT OF DEPARTURE

For those who have read my earlier works, you may notice a shift in tone and pacing in this book—this is intentional. This book is titled *Accelerated Manifesting,* and I feel that it's important to provide an approach and format that resonates with the concept.

I wrote parts of this book for your *unconscious mind,* whereas others will cater to the conscious mind itself; satisfying it in a way that benefits your personal goals. If both your conscious and your unconscious are not on the same page, you will run into internal conflicts and proverbial walls.

The idea behind this book is not only to discuss the concepts of accelerated manifesting—but to allow you to integrate these ideas as you flip through the pages. At the end of every chapter, you can incorporate core concepts into your everyday life and use what you have learned to influence your manifestations, thus speeding up the process. While this is not an introduction to the Law of Attraction (as we will talk about advanced principles); if you're new to these concepts, you can still understand the principles we discuss in these chapters. If certain ideas seem slightly outside of your realm of knowledge, I encourage you to read my earlier works, as they will help you to establish a solid foundation of the Law of Attraction philosophy.

It's taken me years of trial and error to understand these esoteric truths, to work through my internal programming, and to rewrite my way of being according to my will. I hope that by learning from my wins and my losses, you too can reach this level of *quickened manifestations*.

There is a difference between *knowing* these truths and *living* them. This book is practical in its discussion of quantum mechanics, neuroscience, and spirituality—these lead to you understanding the truth behind reality. It's important, however, to make one thing crystal clear; *accelerated manifesting* does not mean *instant manifestation*.

A MANIFESTOR'S DILEMMA

Instant gratification might be the norm in the digital world. However, in the invisible realm, an infinite number of variables influence our manifestations. I hope that by the end of this book, you will relinquish the idea of *instant gratification* and embrace the concept of *delayed gratification*.

Accepting the delay factor in every manifestation is the first step in materializing it in physical reality. Otherwise, you'll find yourself in an endless loop—like a dog chasing its own tail. When you work toward goals and desires, and you savor and appreciate the process and the journey, you get into a state attractive to your desired reality. And that's way better than just manifesting things out of the blue. You might think, "That's not true!" but what would you appreciate more…

- winning a million dollars in the lottery, or
- making a million dollars using your resources, talents, and intelligence?

Which of these two scenarios provides the greatest returns?

Those who believe that winning the lottery would give them more appreciation will find the opposite to be true. Many people who win the lottery suffer from what psychologist Stephen Goldbart calls "Sudden Wealth Syndrome." This term describes a psychological condition in which the overwhelming pressures of acquiring an unexpected fortune can cause emotional and behavioral afflictions. The lottery winner experiences an identity crisis, feels like an imposter, and / or feels guilty about gaining sudden wealth without the exchange of something of value.

According to the 'National Endowment for Financial Education ,' seventy percent of all lottery winners end up broke and declare bankruptcy. This is because, while they were successful in winning the money, they didn't gain the wisdom to generate wealth—as a result, they spent it all. Manifesting works similarly. While it is possible to win the lottery within the context of the Law of Attraction, the source within you in its infinite wisdom would rather have you generate your wealth from within, so you not only win, but you also sustain your wins and continue to grow beyond your supposed limitations.

To manifest a desire without changing who you are in relation to it is like gifting a toddler with keys to a new car. Sure, they might appreciate the 'new car smell,' but the car will be of no use to them. The real goal should be to manifest circumstances, opportunities, resources, and insights that support you and your unique journey and desires.

If you picked up this book to read hype-driven Law of Attraction teachings, this book is not for you. I aim to disrupt your mind, rewire your thinking, and give you principles that work time and time again to *speed up the manifestation process*. So, if you're ready to unleash your power and remove the obstacles hindering your manifestations, *keep reading.*

If you're feeling stuck, making slow progress, or only manifesting "small things," this book will help you. We will unravel your internal blockages so you can *go with the flow*, instead of against it. Remember, direction is more important than speed. If there is no direction, you'll be heading nowhere fast. Think about manifesting like driving to a destination. You need fuel, an address, and a guidance system to tell you what turns to make and which exits to take. Clarity is key.

This book shows you *what is under the hood* of the Law of Attraction and how to maximize your potential to wield it. What would take you ten years to achieve, you can cut to one year or less—it depends on YOU.

THE FALLACY OF OVERNIGHT SUCCESS

American comedian Eddie Cantor once said, "It takes twenty years to achieve overnight success." Entrepreneur Jeff Bezos adopted this adage—he changed it to "ten years to achieve overnight success." What Cantor and Bezos understood is that *overnight success* doesn't happen overnight—but when success hits you and you are prepared, the right opportunities come your way and you grow exponentially. But first you need to establish a foundation for accelerated growth—and within the pages of this book, you'll do that. Manifesting what you want requires you to adopt a frame of mind that stops you from manifesting more of what you don't want. I aim to guide you through the entire process—from the roots all the way to the fruits. If you're keen to achieve your heart's truest desires, your journey begins now….

CHAPTER 1:

SHINING A LIGHT WITHIN

SECRET #1: GAIN CLARITY AROUND YOUR WHAT? WHO? AND WHY?

Did you know you are constantly manifesting your reality? Every day and in every way—you are interacting with your environment, making decisions that either sustain your current life or change it. The Law of Attraction works whether or not you are thinking about it. In fact, most people *manifest unconsciously*. Now, this isn't a bad thing. As long as you are conscious of your unconsciousness, you can use the automated systems of your body to your benefit. Unconscious manifestation works based on *internal cerebral algorithms* written by the brain. The brain is an efficient biological machine that processes *eleven million bits of information per second* and then compresses this data to between *fifty to sixty bits per second* for our conscious mind to handle.

I'll give you a few seconds to process that information.

This means that our unconscious mind—which handles ninety to ninety-five percent of our decision-making processes—is trying to find the most efficient way to solve every problem and achieve every goal. Our brain's capacity for pattern recognition is the reason we human beings rose to the top of the food chain. When the brain recognizes a pattern, it compresses all the variables and writes an automated response protocol—a cerebral algorithm.

The problem is that these automated algorithms might not be in alignment with what you want to manifest and could, in fact, be working in direct opposition to it. *If you do not know what you want, you'll never know where to find it.* This creates conflict and can hinder your ability to manifest. Sometimes, in order to maintain your current reality, it can even reinforce what you *don't* want.

When someone says, "Why does this always happen to me?" it is because these internal programs are manifesting their reality repeatedly. After all, for the sake of efficiency, the brain prefers that all variables remain the same so it can optimize its processing power. Since the brain doesn't need your permission to write these automated responses, it continues to optimize for efficiency and survival.

Your brain is subject to your will, but to exercise your will, *you need to use those fifty to sixty bits of information* to reprogram these automated responses. I'm going to teach you how to build clarity around your vision so you can use this powerful biological machine to write algorithms that move you toward your goals— and how to remove the ones that hinder your progress.

YOUR BRAIN FOLLOWS WHAT IT THINKS YOU WANT...

Your brain is not your enemy.

I know the introduction to this chapter made it seem like your brain is working against you, but your brain is only looking out for your best interests. While the brain is an efficient organ, it doesn't have a mind of its own. Your brain is only putting its efforts on what it thinks you want, and it's only doing so because you haven't told it otherwise.

As noted earlier, clarity is important. Without a clear vision of what you want, your brain can never adjust itself and become an efficient tool for turning your dreams into reality. However, it's important to acknowledge that while a clear vision of what you want is important, it's just as important to understand the *Why* behind your intentions.

Our Why hints at the core features of our desires. No matter what your intention, if you don't know the reason behind your desire, you'll almost always miss the mark. This is because, according to modern-day psychiatry, humans are purpose-driven beings . This innate core need to carry out a purpose and give meaning to our intentions is the driver of all our actions. The more clarity we have around it, the easier it is to support our true intentions with thoughts and actions.

When you understand the Why behind your intentions, it becomes easier to discover exactly *how* to manifest your goals. The outcome becomes secondary—*the path becomes the goal.* What you are doing *now* becomes the object of your focus (as opposed to what you'll get in the future).

When you dig deep enough, you'll never want to manifest anything material. There's always some core spiritual need behind mundane motivations. For instance, when you're trying to manifest money, you might actually be looking for opportunity, stability, or freedom. When you're looking for your soul partner, you might actually just be looking for love, companionship, or a sense of belonging.

When you ask "Why?" for all your motivations, you'll uncover one of these core truths—and that gives you clarity around what truly motivates and inspires you. Your Why is the fuel that keeps you moving toward your destination. It's what allows you to endure "setbacks" and perceived failures, and if you have clarity in this area, every intention you make will have a deep underlying drive behind it.

However, clarity brings additional benefits:

- It helps you avoid distractions—you know what benefits you and what sets you back.
- It separates your ego's wants from your genuine desires.
- It allows you to focus on *right* action, not just more action.
- It helps you endure hardships and control where your attention (energy) lies.

ENVISIONING YOUR BEST LIFE

I'm sure many of you grasp the importance of discovering your Why but have difficulty narrowing it down. In this section, we'll explore a few practical exercises to help you declutter your brain and focus your mind.

However, before we can know our Why, we need to discover our truest desire. You already have some idea about what you want—but if you don't, that's okay.

"Desire" could mean anything. In manifesting, there is nothing too small or too big. In order to create an intention, you don't have to have your entire life figured out. Just look at your current life and ask, *what is something I want to experience more of?* It could be anything material like more money, a bigger house, a nicer car, or something immaterial like peace of mind, a sense of freedom, more energy, knowledge, or wisdom…whatever flashes into your *mind's eye* is more than enough to get started.

That said, you can never have "too much clarity" around your desires. So, to take this exercise to even deeper levels, describe your desires for each of the following categories: Health, Wealth, Love, and Self.

Another way you can approach this is by writing your own manifesto about the life you intend to create. I often call this the Perfect Day exercise, where you outline everything that goes on in the average day of your best life and everything you've already accomplished. Write a few pages to describe everything from the time you wake up to the time you go to sleep. This includes the activities you engage in, who you spend your time with, how you're feeling about yourself, and even down to the most minute detail.

Do not overcomplicate this process. Listen to the subtlety of your heart and focus on simple things that resonate and give you that confident, internal "Yes! I want this." Once you know what you want, you enable its manifestation. So, hone in on your desire. Make it something you know you want now, something you can 'feel in your bones.' Overtime, your desires might change, and this is completely normal. Feel free to revisit this process as many times as you'd like.

You sustain your reality by what you believe, but this doesn't mean you can't get things that exist *outside of your beliefs*. For example, if you have a deep desire to manifest ten million dollars, you may not *believe* this is possible. *This does not mean you should not outline it*. Do not be afraid of writing down the most grandiose of desires. Remember, at every turn, your mind tries to justify the status quo and reinforce known paradigms. It tries to return to its comfort zone. That's why many people who try the Law of Attraction fail—their unconscious minds work against them.

That's the bad news. The good news is that you can change your beliefs. With determination, courage, and faith, anyone can become anything they desire.

"It takes the same energy to think small as it does to think big.
So, dream big and think bigger."
—Daymond John

In order to think bigger, grander, and more empowering thoughts, there needs to be liberation from the 'paradigm shell' in which many people find themselves in. Old beliefs need to be shattered. Throughout this book, we will reveal core principles behind every massive Law of Attraction success story. By maximizing the power of intention, you can take enormous leaps toward your biggest dreams. Once you have defined your heart's genuine desire, we move to figuring out the motivation behind it—your Why.

Exercise: The 7 Levels of Why (The Annoying Toddler)

To provide clarity behind your Why, you can implement a technique called "The Seven Levels of Why" or, as I like to call it, "The Annoying Toddler." Like a toddler, this exercise repeats a question seven times: "*Why is this important to you?*"

You start with your statement of intent. "*What would I like to be/do/have?*" I recommend writing the question down, for several reasons:

- Seeing it on paper helps you focus on the answer.
- Multi-sensory stimuli (seeing it, the act of writing it, and feeling the pen in your hand) increase the capacity of your conscious and unconscious minds to retain the information.
- Writing it down acts as a filtration device for your thoughts.
- Writing signals to the brain, "This is important!"

Once you have written your statement of intent—cue the Annoying Toddler.

Note: Having a friend or partner ask you these questions will allow you to focus more on listening to the answers coming from your heart. Don't get discouraged if you can't reach Level Seven. Oftentimes, your answers can start at the second or third level of the exercise. This means you've already given it some thought before.

Many people who go through this exercise cry a little. If you experience this, do not worry, this is a good thing! This means you've reached your core emotional driver, or are at least close to touching it.

Here's an example of the completed exercise:

- I intend to reach my ideal weight by the end of the year.
  1. Why is this important to you?

- Because I'm overweight and don't like how that feels.
  2. Why is it important for you to feel good about your weight?

- Because I value being healthy.
  3. Why is it important for you to be healthy?

- Because being healthy allows me to achieve more in life and feel better about myself.
  4. Why is it important to achieve more and feel better about yourself?

- Because it makes me feel like I'm being productive and not wasting away.
  5. Why is it important to be productive?

- Because being productive means I'm creating value. I'm living my life!
  6. Why is it important to feel you're adding value?

- Because I want my life to mean something, to create a legacy.
  7. Why is it important for your life to have meaning and for you to have a legacy?

- Because I want to help those I love and the people that need it.

Do you see how this example transitioned from Level 1 "intending to reach an ideal weight" to Level 7 "meaning and legacy" just by repeating a single question? This example shows that a mundane desire will always be rooted to a *deep spiritual need*. If you do this exercise, you too will uncover these underlying spiritual needs—and they will serve as fuel to ignite your journey to reaching your heart's desires.

Your Why will fall under the umbrella of the Six Human Needs (by Tony Robbins):

1. Certainty—being sure you can avoid pain or gain pleasure.
2. Variety—experiencing novelty, adventure, change, or the unknown.
3. Significance—feeling special or needed, unique, or important.
4. Connection—having a sense of closeness to someone or something.
5. Growth—going beyond your capacity, capabilities, or understanding.
6. Contribution—having a sense of purpose, service, and giving to others.

Now that we know your Why, we can define your North Star.

ESTABLISHING YOUR NORTH STAR

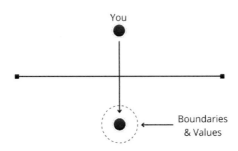

When you understand your underlying motivations for the things you desire—it brings clarity to your intentions. This clarity *instructs your brain to write new algorithms* to get to the outcome in the most efficient way possible. So, it's important to turn vague ideas into concrete visions in all the areas of your life you wish to affect. Otherwise, your brain will rely on its old survival patterns to maintain the status quo.

One way of understanding how clarity gives us direction is by comparing it to the North Star. Polaris, the North Star, is the brightest star in the constellation of Ursa Minor. It is important for sailors and global navigators because the axis of Earth points almost directly at it. This means that at any hour of the night and at any time of the year within the Northern Hemisphere—you can find Polaris due-north.

Defining your desires and intentions is like finding your Polaris—allowing your brain to navigate the dark waters of your mind and guide you toward your desired state. The question is—*How does one establish their Polaris?*

You already have a notion of what you want and why you want it. To create even more clarity, it is important to establish your *standards and values.* Standards and values define what you value the most in terms of your time and energy. Having high standards for yourself allows you to develop an optimized self-image, defining the minimum requirements to carry out the expectations you have for yourself. On the other side of the spectrum, setting limits on what you will put up with is also important. If we allow external forces to have a say in where we put our energy, we end up losing control of the direction our life goes. Establishing these 'energy limits' is a good way of keeping you focused on and standing up for what you believe you deserve.

AngelList CEO Naval Ravikant once said, "Set a high personal hourly rate, and stick to it!" Ravikant is an inspirational thought leader for building wealth, and I like this quote because it applies to the Law of Attraction. What Ravikant means works in parallel with your North Star in that *you establish the rules of the game.* For example, if you were to set a personal hourly rate of $100, doing anything that doesn't generate $100 within any hour is akin to you throwing that $100 into the trash. Arguing with the plumber for three hours would be the same as burning $300. Would you do that? Of course not.

When you establish these parameters, you gain clarity around when and where you should invest your time and energy. You can gauge whether something is taking you toward your goal, or away from it. These are your standards and values—there are things you engage with (as they move you toward your goals) and things you avoid (as they detract from your goals).

Let's take the 'reaching your ideal weight' example we used in The Annoying Toddler exercise and establish our standards and values.

In order to reach your ideal weight, there are a couple of things you could do:

1. Watch what you eat (reducing empty calories).
2. Engage in physical activities.
3. Visualize yourself at your ideal weight.
4. Eat slowly, thoroughly, and mindfully.
5. Watch your portions.
6. Get enough sleep.
7. Find a weight loss partner.
8. Work on stress levels and triggers.

These are just a few examples, but as you can see, *knowing the Do's and Don'ts of your aim will make reaching your goal simpler.* You'll know what to eat, how to behave, and what you won't tolerate. For example, if television advertisements are a trigger for you to eat junk food, you can take action by turning off the television and finding a different activity that pulls you closer to your goal.

Of course, you will need to build discipline, because your body (that is sustaining the extra weight) will fight to maintain the status quo. Carrying out these actions is easier said than done, but there are ways around it. This is where you need those fifty to sixty bits of information, to rewrite the algorithms and train your brain to engage with that which will get you closer to your goal. In metaphysical terms, when you put your attention (energy) on what you want, you increase the likelihood that the object of focus will manifest in your physical reality more frequently.

This extends to all areas of your life. As you can see with the weight loss list above, sleep, mindfulness, and finding a partner are all factors. You need to establish:

- what you'll permit,
- where you aim to spend your time (environment),
- with whom you spend your time, and
- what you'll consume physically and mentally.

It's important to steer your ship toward Polaris—which means being at the helm, navigating the currents of your internal ocean, and moving with the wind, not against it. It's important to define how you'll approach your aim. What attitude do you need to maintain to keep moving in the right direction? What skills do you have to learn in order to move faster? Who do you need to become to sustain your aim? For example, if we're talking about reaching your ideal weight, who is that future person in your mind? Someone who's active? Who knows what they should and shouldn't eat? Who has the discipline to stick to their regimen?

The goal here is to work backwards from where you want to be. When you know where you're headed, it's easier to know who you need to become to get to your destination.

Since we're always in flux, remember to update the vision you have for yourself every ninety days. As you get closer to your goal, you'll gain even more clarity on what you need to do and what you need to avoid, as well as on what you want and who you want to be. This is the Universal feedback mechanism that adds momentum to your journey and speeds up your rate of change.

DEALING WITH "SETBACKS"

Sometimes, when you're on your journey, you may break your own rules of engagement—cheating on your diet, waking up late, or doing that 'thing' you swore you'd stop doing. Perhaps you missed an important milestone or didn't achieve a goal in the desired timeframe. Many people consider this a failure—but failure exists only when you stop trying. When you break your own rules, you're discovering areas in your life that require more attention—ways of *not doing* things. A 'setback' can only set you back if you give it that meaning.

Once more, using the example above—let's say that one day, you had a stressful encounter with your boss. This triggers stressors that prompt your brain to "find comfort in food!" So, in a moment of perceived weakness, you snarf down a few doughnuts. You feel good for a minute, but you regret it later. This happens. But punishing yourself for lapsing into an old cerebral algorithm doesn't help you reach your goal—it does the opposite. Having compassion for yourself in these moments is important if you want to transform your patterns.

This doesn't mean you let things slide—on the contrary, you have discovered that in order to safeguard your future progress, you need to give this issue attention. Instead of feeling guilty or bad, you focus on, "What are healthy ways of dealing with stress in the future?" and then prepare for those instances. It's about proper, unbiased self-reflection.

Remember, your brain is an expert at pattern recognition. It executes its pre-written protocols for dealing with those issues. If—for years—life has trained you to eat a doughnut when you feel stressed, the neural networks associated with this response are strong. Changing this automated response will be difficult at first, but when you find the right alternative, it will become easier to engage with your new, healthier protocol.

As long as you're moving in the general direction of your desire, every setback is an opportunity to refine your internal processes. For manifestation to take place, you only need to focus your energy fifty-one percent of the time on moving toward your goal. Throughout this book, we'll discover ways to increase this percentage and speed up your progress. There is no failure.

WHAT DOES IT MEAN TO BE AN ACCELERATED MANIFESTOR?

This chapter is all about helping you understand the foundation behind any successful manifestation, and that means being clear on three key elements:

- what you want,
- why you want it, and
- who you need to become.

The goal of any Accelerated Manifestor is to manifest with as little resistance as possible. It all starts when you know where you're headed, what directions you need to take, and how to fuel your trip. Many people make little or no declarations about what they want—leaving the brain to write its own internal protocols. As a result, their desires come from external forces, societal conditioning, and old egoic wants. Often, this works against them. Others set specific goals, precise to the last detail, but they also feel a lot of resistance—their doubt is greater than the belief that they can get what they desire.

When you discover your Polaris and uncover Why you want what you want—you'll commit 100 percent to reaching your goal, regardless of what external circumstances tell you. This is because you'll develop a *focused knowingness* about the direction you need to go. You'll move with discipline and won't need internal forces (good thoughts and emotions) or external forces to move you along on your path. Of course, you will experience your fair share of synchronicity for support—but even if that support isn't yet visible, you'll still have your Polaris to guide you.

All you ever need to do is to work with what you know and exercise your power in the present moment. You may not be where you want to be today—but if you're putting out intentions to sustain your ideal future, you're already winning.

What we have discussed in this chapter will give you the clarity you need to move toward your desires, making your brain your ally (not your foe), and assisting you in the accelerated manifestation of every desire you have.

"Clarity is power. The clearer you are about what it is you want, the more your brain knows how to get there. Your brain knows the target and knows how to hit it."
—Tony Robbins

CHAPTER 2:

RELEASING THE RESISTANCE OF NOW

SECRET #2: ACKNOWLEDGE AND ACCEPT "WHAT IS" BEFORE ANYTHING ELSE

While human beings do not possess the ability to fly like birds, the Wright brothers of Indiana used the power of imagination, learned the principles of flight, and on December 17, 1903, they pioneered humanity into the great beyond.

But the famous Wright brothers weren't the first to discover the principles of flight. That honor belongs to a man named George Caley, who made the first successful glider flight in 1853—setting humanity on a course for the skies. Caley was the first to understand the four forces of flight; lift, thrust, drag, and weight. What's interesting about these forces is that they work in opposition to each other. Wings may keep an airplane in the air for a while, but it is only the interaction of these opposing forces that makes sustained flight possible.

Generated by an engine, propeller, or rocket, thrust moves an aircraft in its desired direction. Friction and differences in air pressure slow the airplane down. Weight is the force caused by gravity. Lift, generated by the wings, is the force that keeps the airplane up in the air. Lift works in opposition to weight. Thrust works in opposition to friction.

You may wonder, "Why are we talking about the forces of flight in a book about the Law of Attraction?" Because this example illustrates the core message of this chapter—releasing the resistance of now. Similar to how a plane uses opposing forces to sustain flight, we need 'resistance' in order to manifest our dreams and desires. This may sound counter-intuitive. However, by the end of this chapter, you'll not only tolerate said 'resistance'… you'll welcome it.

SHIFTING YOUR REALITY – REDIRECTION

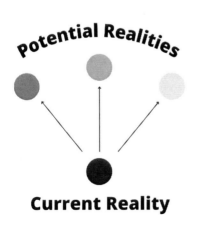

Current Reality

Think back to a time when you were watching a scary movie as a kid. At one point in the movie, the music would build up with the anticipation of an upcoming jump-scare moment. If you were too scared, you might have shut your eyes and covered your ears, avoiding that moment in the movie. Many people live their life as if they are watching a scary movie, ignoring, escaping, and rejecting the reality of the situations they face. Except this time, the monster takes the form of insufficient income, deteriorating health, poor relationships, and many other problems. And when the problems are too obvious to ignore, we attempt to control them with our might and will.

One of the most common forms of escapism is through the use of our memory and imagination. Many people get lost in the past, *identifying with* supposed negative experiences or *reminiscing about* the good 'ole days. Others let their minds drift into the future, painting a beautiful (or frightening) picture of *how things could be*. However, few people maintain their attention in the present moment. To avoid the weight of our current circumstances, it's easy to let the mind take control and project false images to entertain ourselves.

Most people don't like to accept where they are—they try to avoid it, block it, change it—even fight it. They try to escape this moment to experience the next because, within their internal dialogue, anything is better than now, and this moment is not enough. This is where most people are wrong. Trying to escape your reality only serves to increase the presence of whatever you are trying to escape from. On the other hand, the more time we spend overthinking, trying to control reality and force it to change, the less time we spend doing things that make a difference. Reality, as it is, does not change—it transitions.

If we can focus our energy on redirecting our lives in the general direction we want it to go, rather than trying to force "what is" to be "what is not," we can take strides toward the life we want to live.

The shift is subtle, but powerful. It is like Russian mystic Vadim Zeland said, "The stronger your desire to avoid something, the more likely it is that you will encounter it. To fight against what you do not want in your life is to try to ensure that it is present in your life."

LOSING YOURSELF IN TIME

One common way of resisting the present moment, as we've already mentioned, is to lose yourself in time by escaping into the past or future. When you look back on your life, remembering times that were simpler, better, or more enjoyable, it's easy to compare and devalue what you have now. We can limit who we are by assessing ourselves as being the sum of our accumulated experiences—and use that same reference to limit who we can become. The problem with rehashing memories and using them to justify the present is that every time you recall a memory, you alter it.

When you're recalling a memory, you're remembering how you felt and filtering it through what you feel now. If you have a heavy heart and you escape into the past, you romanticize, making the past "more than" what it was. The opposite is also true. We can exaggerate the negative aspects of any event, making it seem worse than it is—or was. Many people who regress to past experience via hypnosis (or other means) discover that what they thought they remembered differs from what actually happened.

Our minds record images and moments, and as we move through life, we tend to filter our experiences through those past events. Whenever we recall these memories, we alter them, adding emphasis to certain things, ignoring others. Remember, we only have about fifty to sixty bits of conscious processing power, and this means the brain has compressed most of the information and conformed it to fit your worldview. Each memory recalled alters the original memory. If you regress into your memories often enough, you can alter your perception—of the memories themselves, and of your current experiences.

Whether you're choosing to live from an imaginary past or future, neither will ever bring the clarity of mind and power of choice that comes when you practice immersing yourself in the present moment. The concepts discussed in this chapter can serve as a pillar for mental and emotional freedom.

Despite all the downsides that come with having a memory, it can also come with many upsides that can support our present-moment growth. Memory can serve as a tool for self-reflection and learning, but only when looked at from a neutral perspective. Often, we have biased and warped perceptions of our past. The only way to benefit from it is to reflect on it as the observer—to not identify as it or see it as part of you, but instead to see it as if you were a third party, separate from the experience. Only from this position can you be open to learning the lessons that the past offers.

On the other end of the spectrum, there are those who dream about a fictitious future—perhaps a world in which all their dreams (or worst fears) come true. Those who worry about the future—about paying bills or dealing with unwanted conflict—suffer from anxiety and stress. Those who over-fantasize about the future—dreaming of a better life—can also experience depression because of how that ideal future contrasts with their current reality. They experience momentary joy, projecting the self into a hypothetical future, only to return to the now to discover nothing has changed.

Imagine it like comparing yourself to a celebrity or sports superstar. Rather than it serving as inspiration or guidance, many people compare the successes of others with their own, degrading the potential of where they are in their journey. This is like comparing the credentials of a PhD graduate with a fifth-grade science fair winner. You can't compare someone's page 300 with your page 30.

That said, looking into the future can be an excellent practice, not only for gaining clarity around the direction you want to take your life, but also as a reference for what you can do now. Seizing aspects of your future-self to embody now is what it means to "live the dream."

While remembering the past or dreaming of the future is not always a bad thing, if it becomes your base configuration of consciousness, or if you live in the past or the future, it becomes a problem. After all, if the mind can project itself into the past or future, it must serve a purpose, right? But if you get stuck in the past or future, you are misusing a mechanism of the mind. And that will cultivate misery and suffering.

If this resonates with you at any level, keep reading. The next part of this chapter discusses readjusting the mind to embrace the "Eternal Present"—the only place that exists. It's where you hold power over your life.

NOWHERE ELSE IS BETTER THAN RIGHT NOW

While your current situation might not seem ideal, it is the optimal place for learning and growth. Nothing needs to change or "be better" for you to take strides toward where you want to be. Instead of waiting for the "right moment," *make each moment right.*

If we can reframe the way we look at every moment of our lives, we can change the next frame in our script or the next experience we manifest. Everything you need to succeed and to manifest your heart's desires exists within the space of *now*. However, when we focus on the future or past, we make ourselves incapable of seeing the subtle opportunities that surround us. Paired with our natural human inclination to view the negative in everything, our focus gets directed toward lack rather than toward the abundance in our everyday lives. This leads us to judge where we are at—and we radiate that negative energy everywhere we go, and to everything or every person we come across.

This energy reflects back to you, because what you put out into the Universe always comes back, whether or not you're aware of it. Shifting your perspective of your current circumstances opens you up to new thoughts and actions that will transform your way of being, thus sustaining the energetic frequency you need to manifest the future you seek.

Every problem in your life is there for your personal and spiritual development. Every human being has a *soul's purpose* and your inner being, in its wisdom, chose this life for you so you could develop on this spiritual path. The life you've experienced so far is not only a mixture of decisions you've made but also a collection of the conditions you were born into (your parents, nation, era, etc.). To some, this idea strikes a nerve—especially those who have endured trauma. "What do you mean, I chose to experience my suffering?" they say. "I didn't choose to be (fill in a description of the trauma)." However, this misses the point. This discussion goes beyond concepts of the mind.

Before explaining further, we must understand the differences between the ego and the self. For the sake of clarity, we can say that these are two separate entities. The ego is a construct of narratives you build from the moment you are born. All our traumas and triumphs become the story we tell ourselves. Our story forms our personality, our internal belief systems, and everything we think defines us. However, as we discovered earlier, our memories are fallible. We conjure up images to reinforce who we think we are—using them as evidence to sustain this illusion of the ego. The same goes for predictions for the future and our concept of "what is." We use our physical reality as a reference for who we think we are.

The self is an entity that cares little for the qualms of the ego. According to the Bhagavad Gita, Krishna explains the nature of the soul and hints at the attitude of the self:

BG 2.22: "As a person sheds worn-out garments and wears new ones, likewise, at the time of death, the soul casts off its worn-out body and enters a new one."

Your ego is a garment your soul wears. At the time of death, you cast it aside, integrating the experience of this lifetime into your *soul's purpose*. The soul chooses the life you live, so it can experience challenges that will allow it to grow on the spiritual plane. You (the ego) have no say in this. In its infinite wisdom, the soul (you) knows that the problems you face during this cycle on Earth are necessary for its spiritual growth.

While this life might seem difficult at times, remind yourself that to it (the soul), it is a mere game to play. This is the resounding message of many mystics, from Buddha to Christ: *This world is nothing but a game.*

Why is this an important truth to learn? The moment you understand that you yourself placed strife and struggle in your life for your spiritual evolution is the same moment you gain power from them. You no longer wish to avoid them. You allow them to be, for they serve as a vehicle for accelerated growth. In this moment of your life, the problems that surround you may seem larger than you. But remember, you designed them to make you grow and become what you know is true within your own soul. Every time you overcome a fear, challenge, or obstacle, you grow. Most people would rather wait, avoid, or look for shortcuts—but that leads only to delay the process or the manifestation of different versions of the events you are trying to avoid. The lessons repeat themselves until you learn them.

There are ways of reducing the number of challenges you need to face, leading to faster manifestations (and we'll talk more about that later on). For now, understand that there is nothing to be won when you fight against, avoid, or hide your weaknesses. When you stop doing this, you'll have more energy to put into improving your life. Not everyone is born with the same mind, body, genetics, and talents, but everyone is born with the potential to live a grand life. By accepting your weaknesses, you open yourself up to compensating for them with your strengths. This is how you redirect your life from the path of most resistance to the path of least resistance.

This is not to say you can't strengthen your weaknesses; you absolutely can. But those improvements need to come from acceptance and allowing, rather than from judgment or fear.

Desires, wants, needs—they all serve a purpose. Think of it this way: you are a manifestation of consciousness that will never repeat itself in this time and space. All of your problems are yours and only you can overcome them. Isn't that amazing? Your problems are your teachers. They are catalysts for the internal growth required to sustain growth in your external reality. As the Hermetic Text *The Emerald Tablet* states, "As above, so below. As within, so without."

There is a subtle nuance to every problem every person faces. No two people can solve their problems in the same way, even if on the surface those problems look the same. For example, say you wanted to learn how to play tennis like Roger Federer. No matter how many times you mimic his swing or how many lessons you have with him, you'll never be able to swing the racket like Roger does. You can certainly get better, but to become the best, techniques, methods, and coaching will not suffice. You need to learn from *experience*, becoming the best version of *you*, and not the watered-down replica of someone else. This is to say, only you can find the optimal answer to the problems you face.

While this may sound simple on paper, it can seem difficult. The good news is, it gets easier. If you want real, lasting change in your life, you must become accustomed to the idea that *now* is the best place for you to be in terms of spiritual and personal development. All it takes is a moment of inspiration and right action to start a change that will ripple through the rest of your human experience. Once you shift your perspective, you will discover an innate power that can transform your world.

This is *the power of choice*. The ability to place your energy and focus on what you want and on who you want to become—and on the unfolding of it all. There are two aspects to this: attention and meaning. When we choose where we place our attention and what meaning we give to circumstances, we're choosing the general direction of our lives. Simple. When you become a master at this, life changes in ways you can't even imagine—and faster than you thought possible.

REJECTING REALITY – AND THE CONSEQUENCES

Now that we have established the reasons behind your current life circumstances, it's important to address what happens when one rejects their reality. That might seem like an odd concept, for "How can you reject reality?" But you'd be surprised how many people live their entire lives this way. There are many ways to numb your senses or to fool the mind in order to avoid conflict, discomfort, or change. In fact, we are experts at it.

We've already addressed two effective ways of rejecting one's own reality—living in the future or past. However, you can also reject your reality through drugs, drinking, addictions, entertainment, lying to yourself and others, and more. Rejecting your reality means going through life unconsciously, avoiding your biggest fears and vulnerabilities, and letting your brain take charge by writing internal algorithms to maintain your status quo. As a result, you continue to repeat patterns your past experiences have conditioned you to perform. The "Why is this always happening to me?" syndrome becomes your norm. Because you repeat patterns, you become fixated on avoiding your life circumstances instead of redirecting them by seeing the opportunities that surround you and recognizing where you need to adjust your life. You become blind to the signs that lead you to a better reality. You feel stuck. You reinforce neural pathways that dictate your behavior in such a way that when the Universe presents you with an Exit sign, you're so entrenched with your automated reactions, you don't notice it. By reinforcing your "stuck ways," you continue to manifest that which you do not want to manifest. As we mentioned in Chapter One—you're always manifesting. Do you really want to maintain the status quo?

THE UNCONSCIOUS DISTRACTIONS OF AUTOMATION

When you enter a state of automation—being unconscious about your responses to life—the information being spammed into your field of awareness can distract you. This "reality spam" can come from two sources:

1. the Internal World, or
2. the External World.

When you engage with life in an unconscious state, it's easy to get caught up in the self-generated narratives of your internal world. It happens to us all. For example, let's say you and a coworker get into a heated debate. You both leave pretty steamed. Even though you are no longer debating, you continue to come up with arguments and talking points—you're still invested, but it's all happening in your head. This occurs with our fears, fantasies, and internal narratives all the time. If you remain unconscious, they distract you from what's transpiring now. Then, in order to stop the noise in your head, you get caught in a game of external distractions. Movies, games, drugs, people, social media, politics—these keep your attention focused on everything but yourself. These distractions steal time and energy you could use to manifest your desired reality.

The crazy part is that the more you remain unconscious, the easier it becomes to stay unconscious. People have lost years by engaging in the fantasy of "what if's" when they have all the power to change their reality in the *now*.

MISSING CUES FROM THE UNIVERSE

Another side effect of being unconscious is not being able to see the breadcrumbs the Universe leaves on the path to your desires. Because your internal and external worlds distract you, you look for supporting evidence to suit your narrative. After all, if you've invested time in a particular thought or action, you're going to want to justify it. At least this is what the ego does when it's on autopilot.

The Universe is always sending you cues, giving you hints and opportunities for significant change. But if you're locked in an internal or external narrative, you won't see them. As a practical example, try this exercise:

Exercise: Everything Green

- Step 1: Take out a piece of paper and something to write with.
- Step 2: Look at your immediate surroundings and identify every object that is green. Put this book down now and take about a minute to memorize everything green in your area.
- Step 3: After you finish the exercise, grab your writing tool, and

write down everything that is red without looking up.

- If you did this correctly, you'll realize it's difficult to recall anything that's red. Perhaps you remember one or two objects—but since you conditioned your mind to look for green, you ignored everything red.
- Test this with anyone—the result will be the same.

Living unconsciously conditions your mind to focus only on things that reinforce whatever you want to or are conditioned to think about.

Exercise: Centering Your Awareness

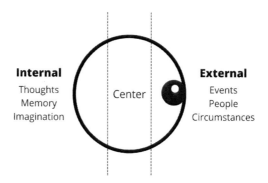

We've established that there are two primary sources of distraction—those of the internal and external world. Most people are lost in one or the other. To speed up our ability to manifest, we have to "disengage" (from automation) and become more conscious of our thoughts, perspectives, and actions. We do this by resting in the space between the internal and external world—the center point.

Below is a simple exercise to help you with this. Practicing this exercise will create a habit of doing "reality checks"—making sure you are engaging consciously with any thought, task, or situation at hand. To center your awareness, ask yourself these three questions:

1. Who am I?
2. Where am I?
3. What am I doing?

Where are you investing your attention? Remember, where your attention goes, energy flows. If you do this exercise over twenty-one consecutive days, you can "install a program" in your brain that starts a "reality check" each time you are about to engage in an activity. In twenty-one days, you'll develop a habit. Repeat the habit often enough and it will become a way of living.

To start, perform this exercise once per hour. Once you become used to this, do it five times per hour. Then do it ten times per hour. You'll get to where you are doing this every time you are about to engage with a task, person, or situation. Once you get used to the feeling that comes from centering your awareness, you can skip the questions and jump straight into the state it brings.

These exercises bring your attention to the present moment and knock you out of an unconscious state, so you make conscious decisions throughout your day. When your attention rests not within or without, but here and now—you don't just take action. You take *right* action, picking up on Universal cues and intuitive hunches that help you along on your journey.

Note: You don't need to hold this state forever. It's okay to choose to engage in an activity unconsciously or "get lost in the moment," especially when ideas, joy, or momentum are flowing. The fundamental premise behind this exercise is that you perform it before making a choice, so the choice you do make is a conscious one. Try it.

THE AIM IN EVERY MOMENT

It's important to *be present* and mindful throughout your day because it is within the present moment that you carry with you the power of choice. With this power, you can choose the next decision you're going to make in your life. This is the starting point of shifting your reality. When you take back your power of choice, you can either choose to do what you've always done or choose to do what needs to be done to achieve your goals, regardless of whether you "feel like it."

One way you can frame this is to *use every moment as an opportunity for growth*. This means making decisions that lead to expanding your comfort zone. The decisions you make, followed by definitive action and unwavering faith, can set in motion an avalanche of change, altering your life forever and accelerating your internal growth.

Are you looking for opportunities to grow at every moment? Lack of growth is one of the main contributing factors to feeling "stuck." To be unwilling to grow beyond your constraints is to conform—in a manner of speaking—to your limitations. This is why growth can often feel uncomfortable. It disrupts what you've always thought to be true about yourself and your reality. It is a paradigm-shattering experience. So, if you want to have the life you've always dreamed of, it's going to require commitment. This means *doing the work*. For many people, this acts as a deterrent (and it is).

Reality will always tests your resolve, making sure that whatever you want is something you actually *desire*. It's the filtering process that makes sure you know which dreams are worth pursuing and which are not. Sometimes the path to getting what you want seems rife with obstacles, but if you shift your perspective, you can see these obstacles are not so much impeding your forward progress as they are helping you define what you want. In some ways, they are forcing you to "think outside the box" so you can grow into the person who is in alignment with your desires. So, it's not always a matter of "enduring the trials" on the path to realizing your dreams, as much as it is embracing the lessons.

Growth is about experiencing new things, challenging your patterns, and venturing into areas outside your comfort zone. It's about pushing your conditioned boundaries and dissolving your core beliefs about self. This can be exciting, exhilarating, and enjoyable—if your mind and heart are in the right place. If you move toward growth, you'll find the novelty of it quite fulfilling. On the other hand, if you try to avoid growth, reality will force it upon you until you open up to it. Think of it like the Universe nudging you towards the direction most beneficial to you.

The Universe is ever expanding. This means it is never stagnant. Therefore, to move in a direct tangent with the flow of the Universe is to either be growing or dying. Either end of the spectrum is valid. However, many people, because of their tendency to generate attachments, want things to stay the same, or at the very least, to change at a rate they can keep up with. This leads to resistance, as we'll always be experiencing change in some form or another, regardless of whether we want it.

To not be in a state of flux consciously is to resist the Universe itself. This is why aiming for growth is so important. Now, what does growth look like? How can we measure it?

WHAT GROWTH LOOKS LIKE – AND HOW TO ACHIEVE IT

Growth is a broad term to describe a limitless process. So, I've decided to break it down into three different forms: Consciousness Growth, Clarity Growth, and Intellectual Growth.

- Consciousness Growth:
  We measure consciousness growth by how much control we have over our attention. We've already hinted at the idea of the power of choice, and this is where we measure how well you can use it. What percentage of your day do you spend being absorbed by what's around or within you? Developing your focus and present moment awareness is key for consciousness growth.

- Clarity Growth:
  Another form of growth, hinted at in Chapter 1, is gaining more clarity around what you want, why you want it, and who you need to become to have it. The more we expand our comfort zone, the more we gain new information and insights

about our strengths and weaknesses. The more we know ourselves, the easier it is to navigate through life, because you'll know the best decisions to make at every moment.

- Intellectual Growth:
  The more reference experiences we have, the easier it is to develop what we call specific knowledge. Specific knowledge is knowledge that can't be taught, it must be experienced. Hence, the more we experience life, the more specific knowledge we're able to develop. This is one of the most powerful forms of growth.

Now that we've illustrated the different shapes growth can take, it's time to look at how we can achieve growth in these areas. For simplicity's sake, I've also broken this down into three different categories: Self-Reflection, Comfort Zone Expansion, and Conscious Filtering.

- Self-Reflection:
  This is the process through which we reevaluate our thoughts, emotions, and behaviors to optimize them in order to match the "way of being" of our desired future-self. When we discover what triggers us, why it triggers us, and how to shift our perspective so it no longer triggers us, we build up resilience. When we transform our responses to external stimuli, we're transforming who we are being.

- Comfort Zone Expansion:
  To push past your comfort zone is one of the fundamental principles we will explore throughout this book. To live an

accelerated life, we need to become more in tune with every aspect of reality. This way, no matter what comes our way, we'll always be able to maintain an objective approach, even to life's toughest challenges. Of course, we're not robots, so this won't be the case most of the time. However, the more we practice this, the easier it becomes to make decisions that lead to the manifestation of your desires.

- Conscious Filtering:
  Changing your environment and the information you consume daily is one of the most powerful ways of transforming what goes on inside your head. Believe it or not, your subconscious and unconscious minds are collecting and storing information from your physical reality constantly. This happens beyond your conscious awareness. There is no way to stop your brain from capturing information, compressing it, and sprinkling it on all the decisions you make. However, by changing what you allow to enter your consciousness, you change where your insights, hunches, and reasoning come from.

THE BALANCE BETWEEN GROWING AND BEING

The concept that you should always aim for growth coincides with society's hustle culture. Many people think growth comes from pushing yourself to act, achieve, accomplish, and "get it done." However, this is not always the case—growth can also arise from *doing nothing*. You can grow by *allowing* yourself to grow. Simply *being*, in the moment, can signify growth.

Growth does not always result from action or discomfort. Becoming aware of your senses or developing keen intuition are powerful ways to grow. So, become an active participant in your life. Acknowledging your *beingness* is an often-overlooked form of growth. Step into the observer role. It's okay to be human. Let go. Enjoy the ride. Your life is yours. Celebrate every opportunity for joy, love, and goodness. The more you live in the present, the more you'll realize that these glorious moments exist in all things—all the time. It's a matter of switching off autopilot mode, taking the helm, and steering your own ship. Sometimes, this means dropping the anchor and taking a rest.

If you're reading this book, you're probably aware of how detrimental living unconsciously can be. But after reading this chapter, you know how to live your life on "manual drive." Acknowledge your circumstances, accept where you are, and allow things to unfold—then you can make your intentions clear and shift the direction your life is headed. As we'll learn in the next chapter, it is within this space of having clear intentions that you can effect genuine change.

For now … close this book…
Take a Deep, Mindful Breath …
In… and … Out...

CHAPTER 3:

BECOMING A PROACTIVE MANIFESTOR

SECRET #3: TURN DESIRES INTO INTENTIONS

Most people have a solid understanding of what they desire (especially after having read Chapter 1). People who use Universal systems like the Law of Attraction typically express desires for more money, better health, relationships, and sometimes, just peace of mind. The way they intend to manifest these desires varies.

How do you intend to manifest your desires? Are you fixated on contemplating the object of your desire? Or are you just loving the *desiring* part? It's important to reflect on this because it's where the vast majority of people who practice manifestation get it wrong. There's an underlying (and dangerous) idea that the Law of Attraction is about knowing what you want, and that by wanting it enough, the Universe will cater to your desires. But if this were true, you wouldn't be reading this book, would you?

"A dream or a wish does not qualify as a choice.
Dreams do not come true."
– Vadim Zeland

If "imagining an outcome" is all it takes to manifest your heart's desires—everyone would always get everything they wanted. The problem with this erroneous mindset is that by fixing your thoughts on manifesting your desires—or on lusting for the desire itself—you are *resetting the manifestation* and bringing it back to square one. The Universe does not operate linearly. It's not an ask-today/receive tomorrow scenario. There are complex mechanisms at work in the web of life as you create your ideal reality, and if you keep contemplating the object of your desires, and working out how it's going to manifest, you're not manifesting faster—in fact you're getting in the way of the desire, delaying it from coming to fruition. It's your intention, not your wishing and wanting, that is the key benefit to being an effective manifestor.

So, the question remains: "How do you intend to make your manifestations happen?" While desire and intention might seem like the same thing, they differ. In this chapter, we'll be addressing what it means to be a *proactive manifestor* and how to frame your mind, body, and soul to speed up manifesting your desired reality.

What's more—by the end of this chapter, you'll know exactly how to make intentions that put you on your path to your truest desires. Let's look first at the differences between *desires* and *intentions* and why you need both for successful manifestations.

START WITH DESIRES
BUT MANIFEST WITH INTENTIONS

Everyone has desires. Whether you're starting on your journey or have reached monk-like enlightenment, desire is a necessity of life. Without it, we would wither and fade away. A simple, practical example is hunger. This innate desire motivates you to find sustenance. If you didn't experience hunger, you would become weak and burn up all the reserves in your body—until one day, there are no more reserves to burn, leading to starvation and death.

So, desire is not your enemy. Even enlightened people in this world desire peace, harmony, and understanding. Desire is the first step in manifesting your ideal reality. It is your initial motivation, your light in the darkness, your guiding beacon. However, desire is also an affirmation of one's own lack. When you say, for example, "I want a healthy body and to make lots of money!" you are also saying the opposite, "I don't have a healthy body and I don't make enough money!"

So, when people remain steadfast in visualizing their desires, they also reaffirm their current state of lack. The Buddha said, "The root of all evil is desire." But I see it more as "the attachment to desire is the root of all evil." When you reaffirm a lack, it creates energetic vampires. These are emotions that drain your vitality—feeling unworthy, jealous, or envious; experiencing self-loathing; being a victim to your circumstances; etc.

If we follow the Buddha's logic—these emotions would be the "seeds of evil" and once evil takes root, it can redirect your thoughts and actions to focus on lack as opposed to the abundance available to you and the unfolding of your desire. *Desire alone will never move you toward your goals.*

Desire should only act as your beacon in life—your North Star. It should not be the fuel behind your movement. The Universe only ever listens to the *content* of your desires, not to the *nature* of them. If you desire to not experience something, you ultimately say that you DO desire to experience it. Why? Because the nature of desire is both a deep temporary motivational pull to move forward and a state of lack and wanting. For something to exist within the mind, the opposite must also exist. Our minds are dualistic, which is why *desire* must be the calling—leaving *intention* to be the primary driver.

Intentions and desires complement each other. Without intention, you cannot manifest a desire, but without desires—intention does not exist. If a desire is in the spotlight, intention is the driver that takes you to your destination. Therefore, to move toward where you want to go, you need both.

Let's look at what separates an intention from a desire. Unlike a desire—an affirmation of one's own lack—an intention is all about creation. With an intention, you know what you want, and you pursue that goal. It's a state of *being* and *doing*, and as a result, it invokes the state of *having*. Your focus is on the movement toward your goals, rather than on the distance between you and them. With intentions, you're not worrying about "one day getting there" but you are seeing your focus, actions, and thoughts as the vehicle already on the road to completion. When you *intend*, you don't attach to the outcome of your action—you shift your focus toward *the process—the only place where you can use the power of choice.*

When you are not attached to the result but remain focused on the *being* aspect of reality creation—you free yourself from the fear of 'not having.' Once liberated from this longing for results, you can invoke the next steps to speed up your manifestations. This is when what Carl Jung referred to as "synchronicities" manifest in your life, motivating you to keep going. An intention is also an affirmation, but it is not an affirmation of lack, it is an affirmation of abundance. Even if you don't have everything you desire, you have "enough to begin." That is a state of abundance. To intend is to affirm that you are becoming, creating, or being.

THIS IS AN IMPORTANT LESSON TO UNDERSTAND. It's also the reason I wrote it in capital letters—to send a subliminal signal to the unconscious mind to remember this truth:

We all have desires, but our desires are the beacons to orient our intentions. Put some focus on your desire, define it well, and once you have done so, focus most of your energy on your intentions to make it so.

WAITING – THE KEY TO PROLONGING SUFFERING

The Law of Attraction has a reputation as the "Daydream your way to everything you ever wanted" Law. This is because the movies that condense these age-old esoteric truths into an hour-and-a-half (and shower the viewer with success stories), do so for entertainment's sake—which can create false expectations on how things work. The problem with such movies is that they cannot capture the nuances of daily life and what it takes to succeed. They need to wrap up everything in a nice clean package. Reality doesn't work like that. Why? Because life is messier than movie-makers depict it. For example, Rocky's training montage took seventeen hours to prepare and film, which represented weeks of training for the character (and the actor). But in the movie, the montage lasted for the duration of the song *Eye of the Tiger*. You didn't get to see the moments Rocky wanted to quit and give up, or the moments he pushed himself beyond himself. You only saw the desire and the conclusion. Instant gratification. However, even within the movie, there is one truth that Rocky can teach us—*"Don't wait. Go after what you want in life!"*

Many people who practice the Law of Attraction do so thinking that all they have to do is visualize their goal, feel it—and the *Universe will take care of everything*. Although this might be true in some respects, it does not give you the full picture, especially if you're looking to practice accelerated manifesting. Little do people who think this way know … *they too are the Universe*. While learning how to master the mind and maintain your emotions in check is crucial to manifestation—it is not *everything*. 'Waiting' is a form of reactive behavior, whereas 'intending' is more about creating and being proactive. If you want to achieve X, you need to create instances in which X has a greater probability of manifesting (but more on this later).

Before we jump into different ways of intending, it's important to understand why people wait. It helps us identify the blocks in our lives and enables us to make the right intentions that get us the best results.

We've already addressed the faulty idea of only 'thinking to manifest'—which is one reason people wait for their manifestations. However—people also wait because it's *comfortable*. The problem with this, though, is that waiting puts you in a non-receptive state. You become unattractive to the desire energetically. "The Universe is taking care of it!" people say, excusing themselves from both the discomforts and lessons that come from walking the path to attaining their desire. When you wait for something to happen, you are not responsible for it. You remove yourself from the potential challenges and tests that lead to growth, which come with the territory of true manifesting. You remain in your comfort zone. The problem is, *if your comfort zone could manifest your desire, you wouldn't need to manifest your desire—you'd already have it.*

This shows that desire exists only in the unknown—a place outside your comfort zone. A place of potential chaos and uncertainty. The unknown is the place where new, spontaneous, and synchronistic manifestations happen.

> *"There are two basic motivating forces: Fear and Love."*
> **– John Lennon**

When you love what you do, no amount of challenges or setbacks can sway you from your path. When fear rules your life; effort, failure, and these perceived 'negatives' become like stones you have to carry on your journey. So many people cling to the concept of 'safety.' Safety is the comfort zone: it's what you know. This is the perfect resting place for the ego and its attachments. No surprises there.

The unknown, however, is the enemy of the ego. When you step outside your comfort zone, you don't know what monsters lurk in the shadows. You can't anticipate; you remain dependent on your ability to improvise and navigate intuitively through darkness. This is scary for many people. It's far simpler to imagine their desire and hope for the best than to put themselves out there and *make* it so.

Stepping out of your comfort zone requires a sense of vulnerability and openness; a trust in yourself and the Universe. It's risky. You no longer have 'control' over your environment—and you stand to lose everything you have.

People fear getting swindled by circumstances or others. They fear being let down. They fear that stepping into the unknown could mean destroying their lives. However, we need to remember that in order to sustain our desired reality, we need to let go of aspects of our current one. To become receptive to what we want, we need to practice letting go in order to let in. If you are waiting, you're operating from powerlessness. You're doing neither. You are not putting yourself out there, testing the waters, growing, nor are you working to detach from your attachments. You simply hope that things will go your way. It's like taking a pocket watch, deconstructing it, then putting it in a box and shaking it, hoping it will reassemble itself. While that's possible, the probability is small. But if you reassemble the pieces yourself, your certainty for success increases.

There's a difference between waiting for a desire to manifest and being patient while exercising your intention. Waiting is shaking the box. Patience is the watchmaker rebuilding the watch. One is wishing for the outcome. The other is knowing it will come.

CREATING PATHWAYS

Understanding that *intention* is an accelerant for manifestation, it's important to identify the distinct steps or actions you can take to open yourself up to more synchronicities, insights, and opportunities. "How," you might wonder, "can I understand this concept in a practical sense?" The short answer: By *doing*. For example, let's say you want to be less lonely in your life. A sense of internal loneliness plagues many people. They think, "If I could only meet my soulmate or make a genuine friend, I would not feel so lonely!" However, this is their perception of *what they think* they want. This is their desire, saying, "You are lacking something in your life!"

After having established their heart's genuine desire—how do they *plan* on making it real? Do you think sitting at home, visualizing your one true love, will make your soulmate appear out of thin air? While it's not impossible, just like the pocket watch reassembling itself, the probabilities do not favor you. However, what if you joined a local club or activity where you'd have to interact with strangers? Do you think the probability of you meeting your soulmate increases or decreases? How would you go about choosing this activity? Would you pick an activity you think your soulmate would enjoy? Or would you choose something that appeals to you? These decisions influence the outcome of your manifestations. Every intention, either through action, thought, or focus, paves the road to your desire, brick by brick.

With that being said, be wary of how you approach this. If you are 'going out to look for your soulmate,' you're still reaffirming your state of loneliness. But engaging in an activity you enjoy, regardless of the outcomes it'll bring, is affirming your love for yourself, hence opening you up to being loved by others. You don't need to look for your soulmate. You can enjoy your life while making yourself available for the potential to manifest. If you create enough opportunities for the Universe to surprise you, it makes it easier for it to comply with your desires.

An intention is thinking thoughts and taking actions that lead to opportunities. It removes the need to focus on the result and allows the manifestor to enjoy tuning into the frequency of what they want. You won't find what you want sitting on your couch, but you're also not going to find it by going out of your house looking for it. The Universe is weird that way—it requires non-attachment to results. Reality shifts in your favor when you open yourself up to the possibility of your desire coming to fruition. Manifesting a desire needs to feel like the normal next step in your life. After all, *like attracts like,* and if you hope to be fulfilled or whole, you have to be vibrating at that frequency already. To enjoy the journey toward your ideal reality, regardless of what it looks like now, is the wisest path.

The real secret to manifesting is focusing not only the mind, but the body, the emotions, and the spirit toward a singular goal—and then enjoying the scenery on the way to fulfilling your needs. It's as much about thought as it is about action without attachment. You trust and know it's already happening—then you focus on your current situation and put yourself in a position to make it more likely to happen.

Think about it this way—if your desire was the prize in a raffle with 100 tickets, and you buy one ticket, you have a 1/100 chance to get it. You have a ten percent chance of winning the prize if you buy ten tickets. If you buy fifty, you have a one in two probability of winning…see what I'm getting at? Every ticket you buy represents a step you took outside your comfort zone, increasing the probability that your desire will manifest.

However, even in this example, there is a hidden factor—cost. Each ticket has a cost, which can represent sacrifice or letting go. The more you engage with sacrificing your comfort zone or attachments—the higher the likelihood you will win the prize. We call this paradigm shift *Stepping into Abundance*—realizing that the prize has always been yours. Now you're following through on the way to pick it up. The beauty of the Law of Attraction is that when you make these intentions and buy these proverbial raffle tickets, not only do you increase your chance of finding the winning ticket, but you also gain more clarity around which tickets (paths) are not the winner and the lessons you would have learned from them.

Through the power of choice, you can increase the odds in your favor. You increase the opportunity for that one winning ticket to fall into your lap effortlessly. Remember, the trick is to enjoy buying the tickets, to do what you need to do to accelerate the process, and to not wonder whether you have the winning ticket but to know you are already winning.

Define the next step you need to take. Create a pathway for it to manifest…and it will be like lining dominoes up all the way to your desired outcome.

DEFINING YOUR ONE THING

One of the most frequent questions people ask me at this stage is, "What should I focus on?" and "What should I do next?" They understand they need to *create instances of success* and not simply focus on their desire. They know they have to do something *they enjoy*, but within a world of infinite possibilities. So, which path is the right one?

Another problem many people face is organizing their thoughts and intentions. However, this does not have to be complex. Certain things can help you decide, among them, thinking "*What can I do now?*" or "*What is the simplest, obvious next step?*" Sure, your desire might seem far off in the distance—but what strategic steps can you take *now* to bring that manifestation closer to your *present moment?* For example, say you're looking to meet new people. This would mean putting yourself in situations where you can meet new people. Taking up a new hobby, going to your local gym, or joining a club are a few examples of steps that will move you closer to your desired destination. Once there, you can be friendly. Smile at people, ask if you can assist with anything, get involved, get comfortable becoming a person who is open to meeting new people. If, after several tries, you still can't make a friend, maybe it's time to learn the fundamentals behind social dynamics and influence. Picking up a few books, studying the topic, and getting back out there would be the best next steps.

These actions live within your *Circle of Power*. Your circle of power comprises all the things you have power over. In every case, it's about how you respond to your circumstances. If you're gripped with anxiety by the thought of joining a club or being friendly with strangers, your next action would be to ask, "*What's the source of my anxiety? How can I overcome it?*"

You are limited only by what you choose to do or not do. *There is always a step to take.* Sometimes the small actions you're taking might not feel like they're making a difference, but you'd be surprised at how fast things change. Belief grows when you take simple steps because these steps move the 'puzzle pieces' around in ways you didn't expect. This is following the Occam's Razor principle. In layperson terms, this principle states that the best next step toward any desired result is the simplest and most obvious one.

Overcomplicating the next step is a recipe for slow movement and delayed manifesting. We tend to dramatize reality and make our situation seem more complicated than it actually is. Once you know what you want from life, the only question you need to concern yourself with is, "*What is the simplest next step I need to take in order to move toward what I want?*" Don't overthink it. Once you have identified your next step, follow through. Enjoy the process. Now you're turning up the heat and speeding up change. Your focus is on forward movement toward your desire; it's no longer on the lack of it or your longing for it. There's no longer this sense of separation. You're closing the gap. This is when your reality starts to fit the puzzle pieces together.

CHAPTER 4:

SAILING IN DARK WATERS

SECRET #4: FIND COMFORT IN DISCOMFORT

The Universe does not favor what we think is good or scorn what we think is bad. It provides whatever we are in alignment with. As mentioned many time throughout this book, reality always takes the path of least resistance. We can erroneously see this path (within our linear way of thinking) as "I want '*this*', so '*that*' must happen in order to make it manifest." We can misinterpret it as "the path of *no* resistance," which is far from the truth. Within the Universal Mind, there are infinite variables at play, not just the ones we're able to conjure up with rational thinking.

There is always a give and take with manifestations. To deliver the objects of our desires to us with the least amount of resistance, reality takes paths beyond the boundaries of what we expect. This means that while a thing or an event might seem 'off,' or 'detrimental' to our vision, it could be a blessing in disguise. It's these alternative routes that life takes us through that I like to call 'The Dark Waters of Reality'—that which exists *outside of our comfort zone—the unknown.* When we wander these alternative routes—*the place where magic happens*—we become uncomfortable; irritated with our circumstances. The unknown challenges the nature of our intention. It'll test to see if your intentions are truly rooted in a sustainable source (your Why)—for if they're not, they'll dissolve or transform, and your path will shift.

For example, when someone expresses the desire to be more patient, they find themselves in stressful situations that challenge the very core of their desire—patience itself. This is because whether you really want what you claim to want, or if it's just a fleeting desire—reality always tests your resolve. These moments are rarely comfortable. They push you to the edge of your paradigm and what you think is true or possible. In this 'no-man's-land,' the true power of manifestation comes alive. You move beyond your limitations and flow with the current (as opposed to trying to control every variable). When you move into the unknown, you give the Universe permission to grant you new blessings and new lessons. But it would be naïve to say that the unknown contains only your truest desires. It contains all realities—what you want and what you do not want.

Only within the unknown can we can play with our human power—the power to choose the reality we want to manifest, intuitively, consciously, and energetically. This chapter is all about engaging with the unknown and tapping into the raw power of becoming *comfortable with discomfort.* We'll address how to deal with the unknown in a way that fuels your motivation, enabling you to go beyond yourself and experience a whole different side of *what is possible.*

STRETCHING THE IDENTITY

We begin with the concept of the ego. *Who are we?* Scholars and philosophers—and every person who has dared to venture beyond their base programming—have asked this question. Are we our experiences? Our behaviors? Our past or present? Our thoughts? While we could spend hours expanding on these concepts, I'll create a base definition for us to build on. For our purposes, we'll define ourselves as vessels for the ego—and the ego as the *stories we believe to be true about our internal and external representations of self.* These stories include your belief systems, values, possessions, and everything you think is *true* about you.

We wear our stories like masks that represent who we are and what we want to project into the world. To a certain extent, we need an ego to survive in this world, for without it, we would be defenseless and incapable of operating in base reality. The problems of the ego stem from the fact that the ego always aims to remain identified, rigid, and static in its nature. What we know is that if we place anything in opposition to it, the ego will fight it, avoid it, or perceive it as an attack on reality itself. When we get caught up in the illusions of the ego, we limit ourselves to its belief system. We close ourselves off to new thoughts, insights, perspectives, and the *infinite possibilities the Universe has in store for us.*

In most cases, the Universe operates outside of the limits of the ego, which is why we experience discomfort. Incapable of understanding how the Universal Mind operates, we don't allow the moment to be what it is. This is to say, we try to avoid discomfort. But in doing so, we actually don't avoid it at all, we only *delay* the experience.

Only through experiencing discomfort can we move toward becoming who we want to be. With no 'new' elements introduced, we'd continue doing what we are doing and manifesting the same things repeatedly. By avoiding dealing with the discomforts life presents, we prolong their prevalence and delay the manifestation of our desires. As the saying goes, *what you resist persists.*

So, it's important to be open to expanding your horizons; to move beyond the limits of the ego. While the ego is an excellent tool to have when you are experiencing base reality—helping you build relationships and relate to the world around you—it always tries to remain attached. This is when we ditch the idea of working with the ego and begin working with our *identity*—how we view ourselves.

The identity, contrary to popular belief, needs to evolve. It needs to stretch and shape-shift in accordance with the goals and dreams you want to achieve and manifest. Within the freedom of a *limitless personality* lies power. This is when your life takes on a whole different trajectory. Throughout the rest of this chapter, we'll discuss more on this.

Although the unknown is where the magic happens, here too is where all the supposed negative situations happen—as tests. These tests can be uncomfortable, but when you frame your mind correctly and allow moments to happen, they become stepping stones to greater potential. And many times, the discomfort we expect to experience is merely an illusion fueled by the unfamiliarity of the moment. For example, a new sofa might have nicer material, a better smell, and softer cushions, but the old sofa often feels more comfortable. Familiarity is the haven for the ego.

Once you accept *what is*, without judgment and allow unfamiliarity to come into your life, your mind relaxes under the weight of the Universe. You *allow yourself to grow into a new way of living*. This is what it means to walk the path of least resistance. By giving power to unconscious triggers and reactions from the ego, you're adding resistance to a path that already had the least amount of it. These tests are not meant to destroy or attack you, but to benefit you. You don't need to know how things will end up; you only need to know that you have control over your choices and that anything that comes because of them is part of your journey. Your job is to focus on the intentions you can place and the actions you can take in the present moment to move things along.

This means opening yourself up to new opportunities, new ways of doing things, and new ways of being, while choosing the ones that resonate with you and your goals the most. When you do this, you open up your perception of reality. You allow your mind to drift beyond the self-imposed limitations of the ego and recognize the synchronicities happening all around you—all the time.

There is a raw power in liberating oneself from self-imposed rules or beliefs. When you commit to what is in your heart and *see the world with fresh eyes,* the world tends to smile back at you. However, many people embark on this process, only to relax when they have achieved a certain milestone. Within the world of accelerated manifesting, we remain in motion, because that is the natural flow of the Universe. When we reach one destination, it is only to see how much farther we can go, while accepting what we have and being grateful for it. There is no end to the infinite Universe that surrounds you—the only limit is what you believe your limit to be.

As noted earlier, when you want something, and when you put out an intention to manifest it, reality will test your limits. The only difference between manifesting it and not manifesting it is how you respond to these circumstances. Will you allow your brain to use its pre-written algorithms (often based on the ego) to navigate the situation? Or will you grab the wheel and steer yourself toward a new way of being, and, as a result, new manifestations?

Now that you are setting your intentions and walking toward them—you have invited the tests into your life. In order to better manage the discomfort and know how to navigate the unknown, we'll be discussing some practical steps you can take now to stretch your identity, and make yourself more fluid—adaptable to the ever-changing environment around you.

We should always challenge who we think we are. It's easy to fall into the idea that you 'know' how things work and how things will play out. This is the ego telling you that the identity you have is fine as it is. Remember, as an expert data compressor—the brain tries to keep things 'as is.' Therefore, if you challenge the core beliefs of your identity, you upset the status quo and invite these 'tests.' The brain knows this and in order to keep things organized, it tries to reinforce what your identity believes. So, take practical steps. Train your brain to embrace and step into change, consistently making it more and more a part of your brain's core programming.

When we redirect our life and change our responses to our reality, we write new cerebral algorithms. Our unconscious mind is constantly refining its processes and when you feed it new data, it expands its problem-solving capabilities. New data means engaging in novel, unknown scenarios that generate fresh experiences and enable growth. This takes courage because it means you will do things outside your comfort zone. It may stir up emotions or old programs you thought you overcame. This is all good! It means it's working. All you have to do is remain in the present moment—jumping into a neutral state and remaining focused on your intentions. Whether it's ideas about self, others, or your circumstances, or it's about personal stories you believe to be true, you need to face it and challenge it with a courageous heart. Why? Because these are the things standing between you and your heart's true desires. As the common saying goes: "*Everything you've ever wanted is on the other side of fear.*" How easy or hard this experience will be is up to you.

If you take the first step in embracing change, you can even make the process more enjoyable and effective. Instead of letting fear come to you, go to the fear. This way, you are in a position of power.

DO WHAT'S UNNATURAL AND AWKWARD

One of the best ways to make your identity more fluid is by challenging smaller beliefs and protocols. You don't have to challenge the 'big stuff' head-on, at first. For example, perhaps you intend to become a performer, but the idea of getting on a stage petrifies you. You don't have to jump onto a stage with a ten-thousand-person audience to face that monster. There are minor challenges you could engage with instead, to build up your confidence. You could start by filming yourself and showing the video to a friend. This is a few steps below standing in front of a crowd, but it builds the notion of doing so. Being vulnerable in front of others will make you stretch your identity. It is not necessary for you to do it all at once. Similar to testing the water before jumping into the pool, you can take small steps. When you've acclimatized to the cold, plunging in is less frightening. By testing the boundaries of your identity, you become comfortable with the unknown.

Are you ready to take the plunge?

EMBODYING A LIMITLESS IDENTITY

When you are comfortable with change—with stretching your identity—you explore the full nature of who you are and who you could be. You realize that if you are malleable, there is no limit to who you are—or who you can become. Your personality can change based on the experiences you incorporate into it. For example, if you identify as an introvert or you fear meeting new people, give yourself permission to interact with strangers more often. If you do this without judgment, this reference experience will change how you see yourself. Your personality will shift. Soon, it becomes less scary to try new things—like going to a social event by yourself, or even going on a blind date. You open yourself up to a new way of interacting with the world, without limiting yourself to labels of being 'this' or 'that.' There is no end to how far you can stretch and mold your identity. You can be whoever you want to be whenever you want. It just takes getting used to.

Many people assume that if you are an introvert at work, you must be an introvert in social environments. Or that if you like to plan your day, you aren't spontaneous. But the traits you embody don't matter; you can change them if you choose. What matters is whether the direction you are traveling in leads to the end goal you want to achieve. To get the results you desire, be who you need to be.

At first glance, this can seem vague, even impractical. But if the discussion is around present-moment energy—the energy required to achieve a particular outcome in a specific moment—practicality is not applicable. It's like saying you need to plan your intuitive hunches or a spontaneous trip. You can't plan intuition or spontaneity. It comes to you in the moment, if you are open to it and allow it. See yourself in a new light, without needing evidence to back it up, and the evidence will manifest. This is how manifestation works, even in the complex dimensions of your personality. Sometimes that means following your normal protocols, and sometimes it means being uncomfortable and facing the strange (internally and externally). Explore that which is not known so you can witness the potential on the other side of your own self-imposed limitations.

FREQUENCY CREATES ACCESSIBILITY

When we look at these concepts from a metaphysical perspective, it becomes clearer why stepping outside your comfort zone is so important. It gives you the opportunity to manifest beyond your current reality. In fact, by stepping outside your comfort zone, you tune into new energetic frequencies that you otherwise would not have accessed.

Embodying a new frequency means you've embodied a new energy. And a new energy doesn't just manifest as opportunities or synchronicities. It gives you access to the infinite information field that surrounds us. The benefits are not just *physical*. They can be *non-physical* too—new thoughts, insights, ideas, and intuitive hunches come when you explore outside of the reality you're accustomed to.

In fact, we can even piggyback off the energy of other people's frequencies, thus downloading some thoughts and feelings they carry with them. Now, this may sound 'out there,' so I'll explain. Energy is contagious. Whether you walk into a room of people mourning the death of a loved one or a room of people laughing at a joke, you can feel the energy without needing to see or hear anything. Once you feel that energy, you tap into the thoughts and feelings that resonate with the situation at hand. Now, this doesn't mean you mentally or emotionally fall into the hands of what surrounds you. This is a natural human response that helps us read situations and adapt to them. Similarly, movies bring out a lot of emotion in us. When we're invested in a character, it can seem like a big win or loss when they succeed or fail. We embody their train of thought in relation to their situation, feeling happy or sad with them.

When we personify a new self, we give ourselves permission to express new thoughts and feelings. This makes identity-shifting a powerful tool for creation. If you can see yourself in a new light, from head to toe and from heart to mind, you can recreate the life you live, internally and externally.

In the following section, we'll look at a few practical steps you can take to tap into different frequencies.

TRAVEL WHEN POSSIBLE

A simple and effective way to stretch your identity is by traveling. Everybody who has spent time abroad will tell you the experience changed them. They leave familiar places and return as strangers. This is especially true if you live in a foreign place for months or years.

Of course, not everyone has time to travel for long periods or the finances to explore foreign lands. Not yet, at least. However, this does not need to be a limitation. You can take smaller trips in your daily life, even going to a different grocery store or spending the day in a nearby town will allow you to experience new environments. Step outside of your normal routine as much as you can. Eat at different restaurants, do different activities. Challenge the status quo of your identity and open up to opportunities that manifest along your path.

When we embody a different version of ourselves, and when we are spontaneous, we tap into a new frequency, shift into a resourceful state, immerse ourselves in the present moment—and open up to new ways of being. With this new frequency, we become more attractive to the reality this new version of ourselves can manifest.

Many people assume that being spontaneous will lead to panic and anxiety. This is a fair point, but only before you've done it. Tapping into a new way of being makes you more conscious. When we are in the unknown, we are more present, because the ego cannot predict what will come next. Introducing more spontaneity and randomness into your life can reduce the worry that comes with becoming a whole new you. Traveling, as a result, can introduce an additional, innovative dimension of life into your consciousness.

METHOD ACT YOUR STATE OF BEING

Sometimes, it's difficult to put ourselves in the state we want to live in. Feeling how we imagine we might feel if we were to achieve our desires can seem like a guessing game. For example, how does someone act extroverted if they've never been extroverted? If this internal block rings true for you, you could always 'method act' your way into the right frequency. To do this, you embody the archetypal energy of a person you perceive as being a close match to the person you want to be. For example, if you wish to become more resourceful and wealthier, you could embody the business-savvy traits of people like Elon Musk or Jeff Bezos. Each of these two entrepreneurs has peculiar ways of generating their wealth. Depending on which of the two resonates with the type of person you'd like to be in any area, you can shift your consciousness to embody their perceived frequency.

Maybe you identify with Elon Musk. First, you'd ask yourself, "How would Elon Musk act in this situation?" Then, by allowing your conscious mind to shift into what you perceive Elon would do, you can reference those actions and do the same. You change the outcome by changing your response.

Of course, to tap into this type of identity-shifting, it's imperative to gain clarity about the personality of your archetype. This helps build a relatable model for your unconscious mind to embody, making transitioning from one way of being to another easy. A key thing to remember is this: We never want to fully act as the other person would. We always want to sprinkle our intentions with our own authenticity. Use this technique to create references for the personality you would like to build. Once you've created a collection of ideal people to reference, take little bits from each of them to mold your unique personality. Like in a video game, you are creating the character (or characters) you would like to play—except that the possibilities are limitless.

In Neuro Linguistic Programming (NLP), this is called "modeling," whereby you highlight the specific skills of a person you admire, then envision them doing it, then you do it as them. Generate several scenarios to practice mentally being the person you're emulating. Since the unconscious mind cannot tell the difference between what is real and what is imaginary, this technique acts as a bridge for you to experience what it would be like to live from this 'other' perspective. You stretch your identity beyond the constraints of your current one and tap into the archetypal frequency of your model references.

So, before moving on, hone the list of people you admire in the areas of life you want to improve. Lifestyle, business mindset, social skills, vocal inflections, body language, demeanor, career, fashion—anything goes. When you lay this out, your vision of your future self becomes clearer. With the help of these references, you can experience yourself in a new state, thus becoming more attractive to the reality your future self can manifest. Remember, it's important not only to think about and craft your future self but also to imitate it. When you incorporate the behaviors of your future self into your life, you'll take just another step toward shifting your frequency—attracting more opportunities and situations to speed you up on your path.

LEARNING TO TAKE THE RIGHT RISKS

People fear the unknown because venturing into unfamiliar terrain is risky. Our minds project potential scenarios or realities based on experience, assumptions, conditioning, survival mechanisms, group thinking, etc. For example, say you don't have the money to pay a bill on time. You've applied for a few jobs. You've reached out to a few friends, but nothing has changed. While it may not happen instantly, your mind—based on experience—generates scenarios (usually gloomy) that could play out, based on how you are feeling right now. The keywords here are "right now." What you are feeling generates thoughts that reflect those feelings. So, your predictions of future events are not based on absolute truths, but on the emotions you are feeling. This is a self-fulfilling prophecy. If you can change how you feel about a situation, you can change how you think it will play out. You'll open yourself up to new thoughts that give you insights on better, faster, and easier ways of getting what you want.

When you stretch your identity, you change your thought-processing norms. Your mind cannot predict your future in the same way it has in the past, because it's relying on data it has not yet tested—meaning that whatever future scenario you might think up is mere speculation, or…it's your choice. For the ego, this is risky business. The ego does not like responsibility.

In such moments, you may experience resistance in your manifestations. When you push the limits of a ten-, twenty-, thirty-, or forty-year identity… rigidity happens. Getting through these moments of discomfort is the key to accelerated growth. As you grow, you become—and you realize you already have everything you've always needed to get what you want.

● ● ●

Up to this point, we have been talking about ways of engaging in minor mental shifts to stretch the ideas you have about yourself. However, in time, you might feel confident about taking a larger leap and might be ready to plunge into the deep end of the pool. But remember, we don't want to follow just any path or have random life experiences. Not all opportunities are the right opportunities. We need to discern which risks are there for our benefit, and which could be distractions from our goals. This is when we look at the difference between stepping into discomfort and stepping into pain.

PAIN VERSUS DISCOMFORT

"Growth demands a temporary surrender of security. It may mean giving up familiar but limiting patterns, safe but unrewarding work, values no longer believed in, and relationships that have lost their meaning."
—John C. Maxwell

To become more discerning, we must understand the difference between pain and discomfort. In our lives, we can't avoid either one, but both dictate how we respond in any situation. First, let's inspect pain.

We've all experienced pain. Pain is an intense feeling of discomfort. It affects our behavior. If you break your arm, for example, you cannot use that arm until it has healed. If you were to ignore the pain of the broken arm and continue to use it, it would only get worse and the pain would increase. The lesson of pain is to step back, regroup, take care, rethink, and heal.

Discomfort is like pain but at a lower intensity. It sits in the background. It is moderate. For example, when you are stretching and you reach the limit of your flexibility, discomfort sets in. A mild form of pain, it's not unbearable, but it's there. It's saying, "you've reached the boundaries imposed by the body—beyond this point is pain!" However, when you relax, take a deep breath, and allow the discomfort to be, you find that you can go beyond this "self-imposed constraint."

The bounds of flexibility your mind imposed were not your actual limits; that was a conservative estimation. When we're referring to manifestation, we experience these supposed limits mentally and emotionally, because most of the time, we do not have physical limits—we have internal ones.

Earlier, we talked about discomfort being a vehicle for growth. Why? Because your comfort zone is a conservative estimate of the limit your brain has imposed in order to sustain its desired reality. So, discomfort is a sign you're on the right path for growth.

Understanding the difference between these two concepts will help you make wiser decisions on your path. It will act as a compass, allowing you to discern between that which moves you toward your goals and that which leads you away from them. Discomfort is the path of growth, whereas pain is an alarm screaming, "Stop!" The more we stretch outside our comfort zone, the more we are one with reality. Only when we accept and can handle all aspects of reality can we choose the best path toward our goals. If we remain in our comfort zone, the paths available to us diminish—and walking the ones that remain becomes a long, drawn-out struggle.

For example, imagine someone who wants to be fit and athletic, but doesn't want to train their body. So, they opt for temporary, superficial solutions, like surgery. Or, imagine someone who wants to have their own business but never takes the steps to learn how to create a successful one. So, they're always waiting for the 'right' opportunity, hopping from one venture to the next, or never learning from their mistakes.

Our comfort zone limits us in ways we cannot imagine. The ego will always create a convincing argument to support us staying within the zone's boundaries. The mind conjures up the thought, "I can do this without doing that." That's like saying "I can catch wild fish with no equipment." Sure, you can, but how long will it take? Better to buy the fishing tackle and become a good outdoor angler—or step outside your comfort zone and do that thing you are afraid to do. If your aim is to learn and grow at an accelerated rate, there is no avoiding the unknown. When you try to avoid stepping outside your comfort zone, you are only delaying the inevitable. You can't hide from reality. You can flow with it and redirect yourself onto the paths you choose to take.

Expanding your comfort zone consciously supercharges your reality. Your intention to create becomes stronger than the limits that are holding you back. This is when your manifestations begin to take form in physical reality. There are two ways of stepping outside your comfort zone. One is through physical action, as we've discussed. The other is through visualizing action. Here is an exercise to illustrate this.

Exercise: Conjuring the Uncomfortable

As I mentioned earlier—the unconscious mind does not know the difference between what is real and what is imaginary. By using the same mechanisms the brain uses to create potential future scenarios, we can simulate discomfort without needing to engage in an uncomfortable action. This helps desensitize us to events we expect will be uncomfortable. Remember, discomfort is a self-imposed limit of the mind. By challenging this notion within our imagination, we expand our threshold for discomfort.

To do this exercise, find a quiet space. Close your eyes. Empty your mind for a few minutes. Bring your attention to your breathing. Once you've reached stillness within, think of something you find uncomfortable. Experience it in first-person. Make sure the image you conjure has an emotional charge. Thinking of this uncomfortable act should make you anxious, fearful, etc. Sit with this feeling, do not resist it.

Once you have locked this mental imagery in place, it's time to visualize how you would respond in this situation if it were to arise in your life experience. Conjure up as many different potential outcomes as possible. Feel it. Bask in these moments until it no longer feels threatening. Allow the discomfort to flow through you and out of you. Don't suppress it.

Without altering the image, see yourself finding comfort in the scenario. In ancient Stoic philosophy, they taught adherents to visualize worst-case scenarios. This isn't because Stoics were a pessimistic bunch. It's because they strove to find comfort in the uncomfortable. They knew that if things didn't work out as expected, they'd be ready. It's this sense of being "ready" to endure hardships that keeps you in balance with Universal flow, as well as in harmony with your thoughts and emotions. The moment you allow yourself to be reactive to discomfort is the moment you lose yourself—in the situation and in your mind.

As you immerse yourself in this visualization, relax. Breathe through the discomfort. Notice how, as you allow whatever is to unfold, you can submerge yourself in the moment, not giving the situation importance, leaving no room for your old self to take over.

This quick, simple exercise prepares you to engage with uncomfortable scenarios in the real world. Of course, it does not resolve fear entirely, but it's a good first step.

BECOMING UNSHAKEABLE

Everything I have shared up to this point has been to help you frame your mindset when the world shakes around you—and it will. Sometimes, who you are now cannot sustain the identity you want to embody, and for you to achieve your greatest desires, you must develop an unshakeable personality. This is when you walk into the unknown, allow discomfort to teach you, and accelerate your growth. Beyond that, you need to stick to your guns; to become steady in the face of unfolding challenges, tests, and events. Committing to your intentions is a powerful way to develop a new state of being, a new frequency.

There's a definition of FEAR I use to remind myself to keep going. F.E.A.R is "False Evidence Appearing Real." It's a story we tell ourselves about a potential outcome. However, unless we try, unless we face our fears, we will never know if we are right or wrong about our predictions. The more you engage with what you are afraid of, the more you realize how conservative you are in your risk assessments. Fear, discomfort, the unknown—they will arise on your journey. They are reflections of the mental and emotional blocks in your state of being. If you learn from them and outgrow them, the rewards will be worth it. You'll pass beyond your limitations and experience life in a new way.

So, when you find yourself in an uncomfortable or fearful moment, take a breath. Allow the fear to come up without resisting it. It will dissipate. If you fight it, it will grow. Unless you are in a life-threatening situation, discomfort will not kill you. It will only challenge the limited self.

Forget the mental noise and emotional triggers, the false projections of potential scenarios—this is all just the ego protecting its habitat. When you open yourself up to your vulnerabilities and weaknesses, you become more receptive to positive change.

WHEN TO QUIT?

It is productive to consider whether the path you are walking is the path your source or the Universe have laid out for you. If a particular way isn't working, it doesn't mean you are doing things wrong or there is something wrong with you. Thinking that could be another ego trap. It simply means that the way you are attempting to reach your goal is meeting with more resistance than expected.

This is the case when you're walking a path that does not fulfill you, drains you of energy, limits your ability to grow, and/or doesn't resonate with the state of being you want to achieve. But if you have convinced your ego that discomfort is growth, it may endure the discomfort for the sake of growth without ever asking, "*Is this the right way?*"

Sometimes, we need to know when to quit, and find a different way to achieve our goals. If you are thinking of changing direction, here are three things that need to be true before you step off the path you're on:

1. You've not seen any significant results or progress.
2. You've given it enough time and energy to see it through.
3. You're no longer excited about process or care about the result.

Only if all three are true should you abandon your course and regroup. Quitting is never a setback, it's a redirection. When we look at it as a new opportunity rather than as a reflection of our potential, we bounce back even stronger. The important thing to remember is that, with any endeavor, *the worst thing you can do is half-commit*. Lack of commitment results from absence of clarity and conviction of intention, which stems from not knowing what you want, why you want it, and who you need to be to have it. So, commit to a direction. Only redirect if you are 100 percent certain in your heart and mind that something needs to change.

Exercise: Shaking the Snowball

Often on our journeys, we'll find ourselves in repeated patterns of mundane days. Either we have noticed no progress or we feel like we've experienced the same day, with the same people, and the same actions for too long. If you find yourself stuck on a plateau or feel you've hit your limit, here are a couple of tricks to shake things up and get things moving.

1. Engage in New Activities:
    We've been talking a lot about expanding your comfort zone, and how uncomfortable it can be. However, comfort zone expansion can also be enjoyable. Experiencing novelty is an excellent way of engaging with a new energy. Take a cooking class, learn to dance tango, or go on a spontaneous adventure with your significant other. In any way you can, introduce novelty into your life.

2. Clean Your Space:
    Your external reality reflects your internal world. Our belongings reflect the energy we carry. Get rid of the old, make room for the new. For example, clearing old, dirty, worn-out clothes out of your closet and taking unused items to the charity shop can make a world of a difference. Understanding

and following the basic principles of Feng Shui can introduce fresh energy to your home or office.

3. Challenge Your Beliefs:
    Study people who hold ideas and ideals that differ from yours. Explore things that conflict with your internal belief systems. Find a genuine reason why people would believe in these ideas—even though you wouldn't—and then test your own beliefs with the same level of scrutiny with which you analyze these conflicting beliefs.

Stepping into the unknown; doing anything outside of the norm, pushes your boundaries of possibility. Your mind becomes engaged and receptive, moving away from that 'stuck feeling.' Simple, deliberate actions is all it takes to create a new configuration of reality. This might be the exact thing you need to open the doorway to your ideal reality.

HAVE A LITTLE FAITH

While beliefs dictate action, faith is a stronger force.

This is because, in order to solidify, belief requires confirmation and proof. Belief is a process, not something you can build up instantly. Our beliefs are constructed rigidly on assumptions we have of our own reality. Faith, on the other hand, has its source in infinity. If we were to depend on belief, we'd never take steps beyond it, we'd stay rooted in the reality we've been living.

In the words of Alan Watts:

"Faith has no preconceptions; it is a plunge into the unknown. Belief clings, but faith lets go. In this sense of the word, faith is the essential virtue of science, and likewise of any religion that is not self-deception."

Having faith in your journey, letting go of preconceived notions of how things should work, and allowing the world to reveal itself without judgment will have a tremendous impact on your abilities to manifest at a sped-up rate. When you become fluid with your identity and can adapt to any situation, you allow reality to take the path of least resistance in your life—and surprise you. And if you aren't surprised, you'll be prepared.

Now it's time to talk about letting go of the 'anchors' that keep you locked in your current identity and reality.

CHAPTER 5:

TAKING THE WEIGHTS OFF

SECRET #5: BE EMPTY (SUNYATA)

On our journey to materializing our dreams into physical reality, the level of difficulty you encounter is relative to your degree of attachment. You may be attached to the way things are, were, or could be. Whenever anything happens outside of this realm of expectation, you experience struggle, suffering, and pain.

When we are born, we have no attachments. We harbor no expectations. Life happens. But as we age, we *collect* ideas, thoughts, feelings, and experiences that enable us to paint a vibrant picture of who we are—or better said, who we think we are. Attachment is the ego's way of proving it is real. When we break or lose our attachments, we experience discomfort because of the 'loss of self.' However, attachment also plays a role in hindering our ability to manifest.

In the following chapter, we'll discuss the effects of attachment, how it creates resistance in your manifestations, and what you can do to rid yourself of the attachments you think you need to hold on to in order to get what your soul craves.

We can begin with the ancient Buddhist philosophy of Sunyata, which represents the void or emptiness of ultimate reality. This means that behind every label, description, or symbol, there is *nothing*. This is the non-dual sector of reality—we are all creations from the same source. The reason this is so important to understand is that when we get caught up in the game of life, we forget that everything we experience is impermanent. We assume things should not change, so we suffer. However, when we identify with that which *is* permanent—the void—we create from a place of neutrality instead of from a place of resistance.

To place this in the context of driving a car, we can say that attachments are the 'things' you fill your car up with—the ideologies, beliefs, emotions, past relationships, and perspectives that you forget to 'unload' before you move forward on your journey. To accelerate your manifestations, you must be able to adapt to every situation, maintaining your core essence while being malleable in your execution. We can only do this when we can discover the power of being 'empty.'

> *"Empty your mind, be formless. Shapeless, like water.*
> *If you put water into a cup, it becomes the cup."*
> **—Bruce Lee**

THE WEIGHT OF ATTACHMENTS

If you think about it, all pain and suffering results from not letting go. For many people, it can also be a source of anxiety or depression.

Attachments are reference points the ego uses to justify its own narrative. The ego keeps attachments in place and the brain, on behalf of the ego, does its best to maintain the status quo. This means that when an 'out of the ordinary' opportunity appears on your path, requiring you to sacrifice an attachment, many people tuck tail and run.

Attachments make you stubborn and closed-minded, and when something new comes along, the ego meets it with hostility. Why? Because from its perspective, any thought that contradicts the status quo challenges the ego's identity—and is therefore a threat to the ego. So, we spend our lives building fortresses around these attachments to 'protect them' from reality. Reality is not interested in your attachments, reality exists. The ego is committed to your attachments—its very existence depends on keeping them in place.

We fear the loss of our attachments because we convince ourselves that we cannot live without them. We gather a clutter of material items and relationships around us that impedes our ability to draw in the abundance we deserve. These attachments are not all physical. We have emotional, intellectual, conceptual, and mental attachments, too. But from an energetic perspective, they occupy all the same space.

Adopting attachments can hold you back from reaching your fullest potential. Remember, *"As without, so within."* A chaotic outer space creates a chaotic inner space. So, consider the sacred art of letting go. Make space for new and exciting things to come along and surprise you. You can't run if you're carrying bricks on your back, and the Universe won't carry those bricks for you. The

Universe asks you to take a leap of faith, to dive into the unknown like a child who plunges into a swimming pool on a hot summer day—fixated on enjoying the experience and the journey. If you're carrying dead weight, you won't even get out of bed, let alone open your eyes to see the sunshine coming through the window.

Attachments can serve a purpose, helping you anchor in a new reality. But because life isn't only about sunshine and rainbows, attachments also keep you out of alignment with your infinite nature. They cause you to react to and be triggered by external and internal stimuli, causing a disruption in your state of being. There are only ever two options—continue holding on to the attachment and carrying those metaphorical bricks, hoping one day they will serve their purpose, or let them go. Unburden yourself from the weight that stops you from accessing a greater field of energetic potential.

The choice is yours.

EXCESS POTENTIAL – AND BALANCING FORCES

Why do we have attachments in the first place? As mentioned, the ego uses attachments as the foundation of its identity. We know that the ego is an illusion; a hologram created by layered life experiences. With the changing of a narrative, we can alter this illusion and prove that (as discussed in the last chapter) the identity we have is fluid. However, in order for movement and interactions to happen in the world, physical reality requires this 'avatar' to exist. For life to exist, we require certain norms to exist.

Attachment is how the identity creates these norms. For example, that sweater your late grandmother gave you or that fond memory you have of a past family vacation form part of the story you believe about yourself. These critical moments in your life define who you are, in relation to your circumstances and your relationships. At least, they help define who you *think* you are.

Without these attachments, you don't feel like 'you.' For example, if you forget to put on a ring you've been wearing for years, you feel naked. If you drive over a pothole in your brand-new Mercedes—and you're identified with it—you'll feel discomfort.

When the ego is in control, it reflects in your physical reality. This reflection happens slowly. While we cannot perceive the ever-changing nature of physical reality from one moment to the next, the rising and the falling or the "wave function" of existence is there. *Nature is always striving for balance*. It reduces the extremes of the up and down cycles of life by balancing out the poles—and to reach equilibrium, it always takes the path of least resistance.

It's simpler than it sounds. Think of a container of water balanced on a wobbly surface. The water swooshes back and forth. However, if we were to set the container down on the floor and leave it, the waves calm and become still. All things in life work this way, transitioning from motion to stillness until they reach balance.

But why is this important? Why do we need to understand this aspect of reality? Vadim Zeland coined the term "Excess Potential," to describe a force induced by the excessive importance we give to our attachments through actions or thoughts that hinders our ability to manifest. Endowing everything we want (and do not want) with strong meanings keeps us out of balance with nature.

From a quantum perspective, this means we are creating an energetic disturbance in the field. Here, the field is the energy and potential that surrounds us. The result? We manifest the opposite of what we were intending. How does this work? Imagine you put all of your desires on a pedestal. The more importance you give a desire, the taller the pedestal grows—and the farther away each desire is. The opposite is also true. If you place too much importance on *not* wanting something, it becomes more a part of your reality.

This is nature's way of balancing the poles and moving toward the path of least resistance. When you let go of your attachment to things you have, want, or want to avoid—you restore balance and move toward manifesting your intentions. But if you continue to place excess importance on areas of your life you want to change, reality will continue to justify that—making what you do *not* want more prevalent.

The key lesson here is this: *You can only create the reality you want when you can accept it as the normal next step in your life and accept everything else that comes in between without judgment.* Attachments hold your manifestations hostage. Once you understand this and embody this principle, it'll revolutionize your life.

REDUCING IMPORTANCE

How does one reduce the significance of a desire? How does one become non-attached? After all, it is through attachment that we construct our identity. Some attachments are so ingrained into who we think we are that imagining our lives without them feels impossible. However, as you'll learn in this book, when you trust that the Universe has your best intentions in mind, you can unravel yourself from that which you do not want.

There is no single answer to the question, "How can I let go of attachment?" There are many methods, and I've outlined three main ones below.

1. Create a Plan-B

   People get attached to their desires because that is ALL they are hoping to achieve. If only they could have this one thing—everything would be perfect. Except … well … we know it wouldn't, and we know that life might even manifest your sincerest desire in a manner that differs from what you expect. So, it's beneficial to have a back-up Plan-B, or even a Plan-C. When you depend on or attach to a single-outcome scenario, you stay out of balance with the possibility of its manifestation.

2. Accept All Possibilities

   Sometimes, you'll fail. Sometimes you'll knock it out of the park. If you're okay with both extremes, nothing will surprise you. All possibilities might lead toward your goal, not just the one you've envisioned. Even what you perceive as a failure could be the Universe guiding you toward a better path, to help you bring your desire to fruition. If you can understand that, even a loss is a win—you can't lose.

3. Do More > Think Less

   Have you ever run circles around a situation? If you have, you'll know that an excellent rule of thumb is to 'Do' as opposed to 'Think.' Within the landscape of the mind, we have so many options and an infinite number of "what ifs," they can render us inactive. We can get analysis paralysis; causing us to overthink situations and imbue them with excess importance. To engage in accelerated manifesting, you need to get your hands dirty. Dive into the deep end and swim. If you're in deep water, thinking about how to swim will never get you as far as swimming and learning on the way.

These three methods may seem simple on paper, but if you apply them, you'll find yourself no longer swayed by external circumstances. Untangling yourself from your attachments can often be difficult. However, it is paramount that you challenge your attachments, ungluing yourself from the illusion of 'self' coming from the ego. To remain in balance energetically with every thought, person, or thing you conjure up in your mind or witness in physical reality is the goal. The more neutral you are about reality, the less its tests sway you. Allow everything to be as it is and choose to move toward your desires. Reducing importance generates two effects:

1. Dissolving Desire

    Once you reduce the importance of your desires, you may realize that what you thought you wanted wasn't what you actually wanted or needed—and that rather than providing the fulfillment you're seeking, getting what you wanted will simply bring another form of attachment. You can build more clarity around what you want when you reduce the importance levels you have for your goals.

2. Quickening Manifestations
    Since you don't hold any specific attachment to your desire, reality can deliver it in the most efficient manner possible—answering the core of your request with the least resistance based on where you are at on your journey.

Reducing the importance you place on reality can be a personal development 'hack.' The moment you take back your power (as opposed to giving it away) is the moment you have control of your state, and as a result, control over the direction in which you are headed.

EXCESS SURRENDER

On the extreme opposite of Excess Importance we find Excess Surrender. Some practitioners believe this is the same as not being attached to outcomes—but it's not. Excess surrender is more like apathy. Here, we call it *detachment*. This is not the same as non-attachment, because when you go to the opposite extreme of desire, you eliminate the need for the desire all together. Excess surrender renders you incapable of manifesting or getting the job done because you never set intentions.

Developing patterns of excess surrender is the same as waiting for things to happen. We call this passivity, as opposed to non-attached action. Non-attachment doesn't mean sitting back, doing nothing. It means you trust and harmonize with the Universe in such a way that you know everything is going according to plan, regardless of the results of the actions you take. Excess surrender creates no true intention, so there is no stimulation to create a new reality. We can compare this to the concept of "wishful thinking," wherein you imagine a potential scenario in your head, but have no intention of bringing it into physical existence.

If there is no intention, there is no response. *Oscillation is the nature of the Universe itself*— at least within the parameters of physical reality. Therefore, in order to manifest anything at an accelerated rate, you cannot rest in complete, total surrender. *Meet the Universe halfway*. Move toward what you know you want with passion and vigor. Every day is a new opportunity to manifest your ideal life into being.

Passivity breeds resistance.

THREE THINGS TO LET GO OF

Knowing that *intention* is the kindling for manifesting desire and *attachment* is the charcoal that dampens the fire, there are a few things we can let go of to strengthen our practice of non-attachment.

1. Control
   Someone who wants to control every situation is petrified of change or of not being in control. They embed themselves in their conceptual realities—believing that if someone/something else interferes with their alleged harmony, it will create resistance, and thus prolong the process of manifesting their desires. When you realize there are infinite possibilities for how things could work out, you discover how little control you have over any circumstance. Wanting to control every little thing in your life opposes reality itself. We cannot control

what the weather will be like tomorrow, but we can control what type of clothes we wear to adapt to it.

2. Assumptions

Often, we assume life has to happen in a specific way. We believe (according to our subjective positions) that all existence must follow our expectations. However, such assumptions are attachments to what we perceive "normal reality" to be. They are inspired by our upbringing, what we've been taught, and so forth. Assumptions stem from belief, and belief is a rigid construct that comes from the ego. Assumptions result from a lack of deductive reasoning, which will always lead to a biased decision, whether that happens in the mind's realm or in your physical environment.

3. Identification

Falling in line with our assumptions is following our ego. Who we *think* we are isn't who we *are*, or could be. Many people go through life attached to the identity they grew up with (or attached to the identity their family and friends see). However, to get to where you want to be, you need to let go of some aspects of the "old" you. Holding on to the "old" you is like holding on to the character traits of the protagonist of a TV series in Season 1 when that character is now in Season 10. Change and evolution are inevitable. Use them to your advantage to grow and develop your way into the reality you want to experience. Learn to be adaptable, soft, and dynamic. Be like water—move in tandem with the flow.

Life has similar properties to water. Water is formless—no matter what container you put it in, it fits. Your creative consciousness is like the ocean, and your beliefs are like water in a cup. When your creative consciousness is still, you can reflect your internal desires with crystal clarity. However, attachments, assumptions, and assertions of control are all ripples that interfere with the clarity of the reflection. The harder you try to control the ripples, the more you disturb the water and the more chaotic the image becomes.

Non-attachment is the only way to bring the reflected image back to stillness and clarity. You must allow the ripples to be while accepting your current state of being. In order to not disturb the water, you must become the water. Then, life flows.

JUST LET BE

Non-attachment is about removing your resistance to your current, past, and potential future circumstances. It's one of the many paths to enlightenment and will increase the likelihood of manifesting your desires.

It might seem paradoxical to think that one must let go of the importance of their desire while remaining focused on bringing it to fruition. However, it's not about obliterating your internal wants and desires. It's about letting go of what you think the answer should be. It's about embracing the fact that the Universal Mind is equipped to find efficient, beneficial means of delivering your genuine desires. It's about unburdening yourself, leaving behind the weights that impede your forward progress, and freeing yourself from self-imposed constraints.

Once you master the art of letting go, you see opportunity and beauty in every situation. The concepts of 'good experience' and 'bad experience' become a part of a *whole experience* and no longer require arbitrary definitions. Become a true manifestor. Let go of things that are holding you back. This doesn't mean you need to burn all your possessions, shave your head, or meditate in the mountains twelve hours a day. It means that when you feel stuck, uncomfortable, challenged, or tested, ask yourself, "*What am I holding on to? What is bringing up this discomfort? What can I do to redefine the situation? How can I develop beyond my current (supposed) limitations? How can I allow this moment to just be, without avoiding it, fighting it, or resisting it?*"

Non-attachment will accelerate your ability to manifest and expand the magnitude of your future manifestations.

CHAPTER 6:

BEAUTIFYING YOUR PHYSICAL REALITY

SECRET #6: ONLY LOOK FOR WHAT YOU WANT TO FIND

"What the Thinker Thinks, the Prover Proves"
—Robert Anton Wilson

D o you remember what it felt like to be a kid? The world was our playground. At school, at home, outside, we made the most out of every situation. We turned furniture into rocks and the living room floor into molten lava. We'd play cops and robbers. Adults hid candy, and we'd become scavengers looking for treasure. We'd transform our physical reality. We were the ultimate alchemists—we would *bring life to life*. But as we grew older, we lost touch with that which made living so enjoyable. We played adult games instead—carrying our failures, supposed limitations, and material belongings on our back everywhere, making life feel heavier as the days went by.

You now have tools to help you let go of some of that baggage. Once you become non-attached to that which holds you back, it's time to beautify your reality, like you used to do when you were a kid. Within every moment, all possibilities exist, both what people perceive to be 'good' or 'bad' (or, in better words, the positive and negative perceptions of reality). This is best illustrated by the black and white symbol that represents the Yin and Yang of life.

In the previous chapter, we focused on attachments and how they create additional resistance. Now we'll examine how you can shift your mind to look for and create positive signs that your intentions are coming to fruition. The more we practice seeking and creating these confirmations, the easier it becomes to identify them. To explain this phenomenon, famed author Robert Anton Wilson called this the "Prover" proving what the "Thinker" thinks. The "Thinker" is your conscious mind—the fifty to sixty bits of information you're working with, and the "Prover" is the unconscious mind that reorganizes itself to ensure that what you focus on manifests more frequently. When you look for confirmations of your intention manifesting, the brain accesses the ten million bits of information your unconscious mind processes and redirects the compression of this information to supply you with evidence that you are moving in the right direction. It allows your fifty to sixty bits of information to pick up on the 'proof.'

Every time you uncover a confirmation, your discovery revitalizes your motivation; it compels you to keep moving. If you find evidence that you're "not achieving" your objectives, that can detract from your motivation, making it more difficult for you to continue moving forward with intention. Therefore, in this chapter, we'll look at why it's important to seek confirmation that your desires are manifesting and look for practical ways you can train your brain to become a master at finding the right confirmation in all situations.

We'll inspect why it's important for you to surround yourself with positive energy and to create a "filtered experience of benefit" by finding the positive in all events—even those that feel negative. We're going to learn how to take these positive confirmations and use them to shift your mind from believing something is working to *knowing* it is—which, when practiced enough, will increase your conviction and confidence with every decision you make.

To begin, we'll go over the importance of a mental diet and how what you consume physically, mentally, emotionally, and spiritually either accelerates your path or creates resistance.

WATCH WHAT THE EYE IS SEEING...

Jesus once said,

"The lamp of the body is the eye. If your eye is good,
your whole body will be full of light. But if your eye is bad, your
whole body will be full of darkness."
— Matthew 6:22-23

You become what you focus on and what you allow to enter through the senses, meaning that what you see, hear, and engage with plays a pivotal role in your personal transformations. So, it's important to guard the senses and choose wisely what you allow your mind to focus on, because (as we discussed at the beginning of this chapter), "What the Thinker thinks…." Therefore, if you are seeing the negative or surrounding yourself with people who perpetuate negativity, it's easier for your mind to fill with negative thoughts, perspectives, and beliefs. The more you focus on it, the more the Prover proves it so.

If your eye is bad, the whole body will be full of darkness. "Darkness" in this case refers to negative perceptions of 'what is'—framing your mind and body to follow suit. No matter where you are in life—you can shift your perspectives today to accelerate the "tomorrow" you want to manifest. When you shift your focus onto ideas, perspectives, and resources that benefit you—reality responds in kind.

ENERGY FOLLOWS ATTENTION

Many people believe that "time" is the most valuable resource on the planet—however, for those who understand how reality works, this is not the case. *Time is relative*. This means that for some people, time moves slower; for others, it moves faster. Time is not a finite resource, even though, within their linear existence, people are convinced it is. By reading this book, you are *gaining time* by absorbing the concepts needed to *do more in less time*. If you are open to learning from the experience of others, you don't have to go through the same challenges to reach the same conclusions. Hence the saying:

> *"It takes a wise person to learn from their mistakes,*
> *but a wiser person to learn from others'."*

You don't need to start from zero and learn through trial and error because I—and those I've learned from—have endured the suffering and spent the time to understand the truths I've outlined here. Books are condensed time, captured in a medium. When you allow yourself to be receptive to 'downloading' the information contained within these pages, you add time to your life.

So, if time is not the most valuable resource in the Universe—what is? To discover the answer, consider this: What are advertisers and technology platforms trying to get from *you*? Your attention. This is because *energy follows attention*. It is the reason programmers optimize algorithms to *trigger you* in such a way that something captures your attention and keeps you engaged. If they have your attention, they can sell your attention to the highest bidder. Advertisers pay for attention because once they capture it, they can influence your desires. Before you know it, you're standing in line, waiting for the latest tech gizmo that "promises" to satisfy your insatiable appetite to engage with the latest trend. Missing out on such a big movement can cause you to feel 'left out,' so you hop on the next train when it arrives.

All that said, the reason time isn't the most valuable resource in the Universe is because time only measures awareness. It cannot exist in a vacuum. If there is no one to observe time, time is irrelevant. We use attention to project our energy onto things we want manifested more often in our lives. Thus, when we can better manage our attention, we have more choice in the direction our lives go.

AUDITING YOUR ATTENTION

So, the questions become, "How much 'attention' are you spending on the things *you* want in life? How much of your attention is being sapped by external stimuli?" All kinds of external sources are trying to get your attention, but you have the power to decide where to spend it. Are you spending your attention on manifesting your desired reality? Or are you spending time on things that detract from the person you want to become? If this question is hard to answer, it's a good idea to audit your day or your week and identify (with brutal honesty) how you spend your attention. If you're honest, you'll identify areas in your life you could rework. For example, how much TV do you watch? What kinds of shows do you watch? How many hours do you engage with strangers on the internet trying to convince them of your beliefs? Does this help or hinder your quest to achieve your goals?

Exercise: Attention Auditing

An excellent exercise is to set an alarm every thirty minutes for one week. When the alarm goes off, write down the activity you were engaged in at that moment. By the end of the week—assuming you sleep eight hours per day—you should have recorded 280 activities. This should give you a rough estimate of where you are spending most of your attention.

Once we have identified that which wastes our attention, we can redirect it. At first, it may seem difficult, because the brain likes to keep the patterns it has established. But once you get into the habit of *choosing* where you place your attention, instead of having it taken from you, you take back your power and energy.

Auditing your day to find and reduce engagement with energy-draining activities is a good first step. However, it's not the only stimuli stealing your attention.

AUDITING YOUR CIRCLE

The people you surround yourself with are as important as the activities you engage in. Some might even say people are even more important. These days, many people are connecting through online meetings and video calls. Others prefer the 'old-fashioned' way of engaging in-person. Regardless of which form of social interaction you wish to take up, you can almost always feel the energy exchange between each other. The energy between friends is palpable.

It's true when they say, "Show me your friends and I'll show you your future." When you engage with people who spend their attention on low-level energy activities, you resonate with the herd. Often, this is not conscious—it's hard-wired into our genetic code. It's the reason primitive humans feared being exiled from their community more than death. Individuals are far more likely to perish in the wild than if they remain with the collective. We human beings build community as a means of survival and growth.

However, when you belong to a collective, it also means you develop the tendency to obey the norms of the group. If the group resonates with low-energy-level activities and you engage in higher-energy-level activities, the group may 'attack' your outlier behavior.

Why? Because when your behavior differs, it places a group's consensus and constants in danger, which puts every person in the collective in 'danger.'

Of course, there will be many open-minded groups that will accept and support the 'new' you, but there will also be those who see you as a threat to their status, position, or identity. Therefore, when a person betters themselves, often, others resist the change. If you surround yourself with friends or acquaintances who resonate with low-energy-level activities—consuming negative content, mistreating others, gossiping, drinking, eating junk food, etc.; they can force you to comply with their behavior in order to 'belong'—or they can challenge you for going against the norm. It's no wonder successful people in different areas of life have a 'letting go story' for past relationships. Outgrowing those you surround yourself with is a normal part of the growth process. Don't shame yourself. Accept the loss of friends and colleagues with a kind heart, gratitude, and compassion, rather than with regret, judgment, and blame.

● ● ●

Let's jump into the practice. One of the best ways to speed up the manifesting process is by surrounding yourself with people who support their personal growth in similar ways to you. This is one of the most powerful ways of creating life-changing shifts in your relationships, business, or circumstances.

Remember, where your attention goes, energy flows. Therefore, you can forge the reality you wish to manifest by surrounding yourself with instances and people that confirm you are making progress toward your desired reality. Leave no room (or as little room as possible) for negativity, or for anything that detracts from reaching your goal. Of course, this doesn't mean that setbacks and challenges won't happen, or that they should be ignored. You may have heard of the term "toxic positivity," that people should always force themselves to be positive and never negative. The reason this doesn't work is that *you can't transform a situation without accepting it first.*

As we established earlier, in order to take flight, certain 'resistances' need to be in play. The meaning you put on your low moments matters. It's the difference between *eustress* (stress that benefits you), which you experience when training your perspective, redirecting your course, and/or uncovering limiting beliefs; and *distress*, which is stress that works against you, causing anxiety, tension, impatience, and/or anger. So, create advantages from negative moments instead of forcing them to change. Remember, if you allow negativity to creep into your way of thinking, your mind will find more instances of negativity—and you'll see only 'what you do not want' as opposed to seeing 'what is.'

In the next few sections, we're going to focus on a few practices to beautify your physical reality and increase your probability of success in any endeavor. The following three techniques will fulfill this purpose.

Technique #1: Moving with Love

Rhonda Byrne, Australian television writer of the smash hit *The Secret*, once said, "The feeling of love is the highest frequency you can emit." Love has no conditions. It moves without negative intentions. It gives without reason. It cares without expectation. In addition, as Gandhi put it, "Where there is love, there is life."

I could write volumes about love, but for the sake of keeping this book focused, I'll just provide practical examples of what it means to "move with love." Love is a strong, if not the strongest, form of intrinsic value. When you love someone, you add value to their life. We should add love (or value) to every situation we find ourselves in. First, acknowledge that you have an abundance of value to give, regardless of who you are. Second, know that you can give it without feeling you've 'lost' something. Give, expecting nothing in return.

There's an old Cherokee story about two wolves that fight inside of each one of us. One embodies anger, sorrow, envy, regret, arrogance, self-pity, guilt, resentment, inferiority, lies, false pride, superiority—representing the 'evil' in us. The other embodies positive emotions—joy, peace, love, hope, serenity, kindness, humility, benevolence, empathy, generosity, truth, compassion, and faith—representing the 'good' in us. The question is: "Which wolf will win?" The answer? The one you feed.

Love is the highest of the positive emotions. When you focus on spreading your abundance and love to the world, you feed the 'good wolf.' Focus on feeding this wolf in any way possible. Do not focus on being selfish or selfless. When we get caught up with these terms, we fall into the ego trap of expecting things in return or keeping tabs on people. This is the opposite of what you want to do. Focus on the vibrational increase of everything around you. There is always a way, even if at first it doesn't seem obvious. If a situation is too tense or overwhelming to apply this, allow it to unfold until there's a "gap of neutrality"—the moment where things are at a standstill—and then redirect its course.

It's hard to be still when you're holding a boiling pot in your bare hands. When your mind, body, and emotions are engaged in a particular "negative" experience, it's common (but not wise) to react. Remember, these moments mostly bring with them discomfort, not pain. Let it be. Rather than jumping in to 'accept' or 'love' when you are in a bad state or when a situation is tense, observe what's happening. In time, the proverbial pot will cool down, and you can then redirect in the direction you want.

When we engage with people and situations and find ourselves incapable of interacting with them in a manner beneficial to both parties, we need to create temporary distance, regain our composure, and cool off. When the moment appears for us to re-engage, we can seek a solution in love, and not respond from a place of hurt, pain, or anger. You can do this by ensuring mutual assured benefit where possible. In modern terms, we know this as "win-win situations," where there is no loser within an exchange or interaction. This is another component of moving through the world with love. The more you do it, the stronger the corresponding wolf inside becomes.

Accelerated manifesting can't happen from a place of greed and lack. There will always be a limit to your accomplishments if your intentions are not pure. Having the best of intentions energetically compounds over time to your benefit, leading to the exponential growth you're aiming for. Developing a deeper sense of self-love and an abundant mindset is critical for this step. Without them, you'll come from a place that does not have the same power as love.

Before you can introduce this concept to your life, you must accept your life and be confident about it in every way, even if it's not yet where you want it to be. We're only able to give love when we have an overflow of it. Otherwise, you'll sprinkle every intention you have with bits and pieces of the "bad wolf," making you take actions and think thoughts that come from greed, lack, or neediness. *You can never always have the perfect solution to a problem, but you can always have perfect intentions.* The more you practice the foundational concepts we talked about in previous chapters, the easier this technique will be to apply.

Technique #2: Tapping into the Collective

We spoke about the collective earlier. We know that if we hang around people who engage in low vibrational activities, they will condition us to follow them. It's human nature. But does this mean you should stop hanging around with your lifelong friends? While changing your social circle is possible, it's difficult to achieve with sheer will. Besides, who do you know personally that is living as you'd like to live? Odds are, not too many people.

To abandon your current relationships because you perceive them as "not ideal" might be counterproductive. Therefore, it is simpler to focus on shifting your own frequency first—which will allow you to tap into peer groups of a similar frequency without destroying your current relationships or being influenced by them. This means becoming a person who is attractive to the type of peer groups you would like to join.

As we spoke about earlier, you don't need to find these peer groups within your current physical reality, even though this would be ideal. You can always start digitally. However, if you feel up for the challenge, finding physical groups to join will maximize the benefits of this practice. You're looking for positive peer groups related to the area of life you wish to improve. These groups focus on the positives while being honest about the negatives. Find any group that resonates with what you want to achieve, whether you're talking about people already accomplished in an area you wish to improve, or others who are also on a similar journey to you. The former will usually come as a coach or mentor, while the latter will involve masterminds or peer groups.

Ideally, you'd like to be the 'least qualified' in any group you are in because that way, there are others you can learn from. If you are the 'most qualified' or the 'most accomplished' in any area, it can be more difficult to grow. That said, there are mixed cases, in which the hierarchy of success within a group doesn't apply because everyone brings their unique value to the table.

The most important aspect of any group is that you trust and support each other, while maintaining a steady rate of growth and valuable contribution between all members. Having a group like this forces you to want to develop yourself to keep up with the dynamics. If you can put yourself in this kind of environment, this can be a great catalyst for growth.

Once you have identified a positive peer group that will help with accelerating your manifestations, it's time to create accountability. Tell the group what you wish to achieve. Be vulnerable. Be open. No relationship is ever sustainable or impactful without vulnerability. Once you've opened up, in most cases, others will ask questions or provide perspectives to help you achieve your goals. Also, stay accountable—you're tapping into the survival instincts of the collective, after all. To not perform would be counter to the norms of the new group, and your mind will be geared toward trying to achieve the goals to accommodate these new norms. Within a positive group, you'll benefit from your peers, and vice versa, and that will empower you to achieve your goals. Others might provide you with tips on managing your time or on how to do a particular action better, or they may tell you what pitfalls to avoid. This will be your chance to provide your own insights and raise the vibration of the group.

This is the power of a positive peer group—do not underestimate it. Napoleon Hill called this the Mastermind Principle, which he defined as "when two or three people work in perfect harmony for the attainment of a specific purpose." Within the Mastermind Alliance, as Hill called it, you can "borrow" education, experience, and sometimes even capital, from those within the group. You become more than your own efforts because people are working in tandem with you toward a goal.

Now, it's important to understand that a peer group might not be a Mastermind Alliance. We might classify a group of entrepreneurs as a positive peer group but it only becomes a Mastermind Alliance when you identify two or three more people in the group who can *work with you* to attain a specific purpose. These are people who have the same (or similar) goals as you. Of course, you have to move with love, which ensures a win-win scenario for everyone. According to Hill, only by attaining the Mastermind Alliance will you be able to get the "Master Key of Success."

As mentioned earlier, another method to speed up growth is by finding a coach or a mentor. These are people who have achieved what you want to achieve in life and who will show you how they did it. The difference between learning from a book and learning from a mentor is that books solve problems by giving you knowledge, while mentors help you solve problems with *specific knowledge*. Specific knowledge is knowledge gained from experience and application. It's the type of knowledge you cannot teach. It must come from experience. And when you have a mentor, it's easier to dissect the subtle nuances of a concept after applying it, as opposed to just logically understanding it. Grasping nuance makes a world of difference.

I cannot stress how important this specific part of the exercise can be and how it can accelerate your ability to manifest. Surrounding yourself with the right people is one of the most powerful ways of increasing your ability to focus your attention on the right things, which leads to the right actions, generating the right results.

Technique #3: Conscious Filtering

We have already touched on the idea of filtering what enters your consciousness. I'd like to expand on that idea. We know that our attention leads our energy and whatever we focus on *becomes*. We know that when we fill our mind with 'junk food' or negative ideas or perspectives, we condition our mind to seek more instances of that—proving what the Thinker thinks. However, when we direct our attention to things that benefit us, we change the way we feed our consciousness, filling it with valuable insights that later can come as intuition or creativity. This, as a result, can lead to better decisions and innovative ideas.

There is an analogy I like to use known as the "Garden of Desire." The garden represents your life. The seeds are the desires you plant in the soil, but a seed cannot grow unless it has water, sunlight, and healthy soil. Thus, when you give your attention to things that resonate with your desire, you are watering the seeds. Sunshine comes from clarity, and clarity comes from reflecting on yourself and your actions. The soil is the environment. It's the people and things you surround yourself with, and the content you consume. And finally, the water is your intention to make these seeds grow. When you have these elements in place, you can grow any desire from a seed to a tree filled with fruit. By surrounding your attention with a world consistent with your desires, the thoughts and actions necessary to make it happen come naturally.

The more fruit you pick from your garden, the more you *know* that the principles of growth are true. The knowledge becomes like a fertilizer you can use in the garden to generate bigger, greater, and faster results.

TURNING BELIEF INTO KNOWING

Throughout this book, we have touched on the concepts of belief and its importance in the practice of manifesting. If you believe you cannot get something, life will prove you right.

A belief is the acceptance that something is true or that something exists. For example, you may believe that the world was formed 4.5 billion years ago. You have no evidence, but you believe what geologists and other scientists tell you. However, this may not be what happened. What if everything in this world, including the evidence that suggests that the world is 4.5 billion years old, spawned into existence last Thursday, along with all your memories and thoughts (and everyone else's?). It's absurd, but this is a mental exercise in absurdism, meant to show you the fallibility of belief.

While this is a fun mental experiment (if the world came into existence less than a week ago, and with it produced all of your personal identity, history, and so forth), there would be no reason to question any of it. You'd observe the narrative presented, accept it as true, and 'prove' its validity. It's simpler to follow what consensus reality tells us (along with what the experts in their respected fields tell us about our origins). Belief can change when core values are challenged. The moment we feed our consciousness with content that feeds our intentions is the moment we can transform our beliefs.

For example, at one point, you may have believed you couldn't ride a bike. But after you experimented, you achieved your desired goal, and that belief changed. Over time, you stop *believing* you can ride a bike. The experience becomes so entrenched in your programming that 'believing' converts to 'knowing.' It is no longer an issue of speculation. You *know* you can ride a bike because you've proven it enough times to make it so.

We've mentioned before that we create our *beliefs* through a rational process within the mind, while *knowing* comes from the heart. Belief is one level below knowing. Belief needs evidence, while knowing is certainty. Before we can go from believing in a manifestation to knowing it will come true, we need to let go of and transform the beliefs that make our desires feel *not* possible. The mind needs proof—so that's what we'll give it.

Let's look at two ways on how to do this.

Technique #1: Positivity in All Things

As we discussed earlier, when you're walking toward a desired reality, you will face resistance. This is reality testing your resolve. It is within these tests and apparent failures that you shift your belief into knowing. The next time you face a setback, instead of giving in to the moment and allowing the negativity of the result to dictate your emotional, mental, or physical state—become mindful of everything. Refocus your awareness to seek the *advantages* of every situation like a bloodhound sniffs out its target. If it's too difficult for you to see the positives in a situation, assume that there is one, and that it lies outside of your current belief system. This is where faith comes into play—accepting there are greater forces at work helping you achieve your goal.

This simple reframing of your perspective toward situations will help cultivate a strong, abundant Garden of Desire.

Technique #2: Confirming the Inevitable

The dominant theme of this chapter is about finding confirmation that your desires are coming to fruition. This is directing the Thinker to look for confirmations and allowing the Prover to prove that they are happening. I call it the "Great Universal Conspiracy," wherein the Universe conspires in your favor. Therefore, find any piece of evidence, irrespective of how irrelevant or small it may seem, that reaffirms that you are doing your part to manifest your ideal reality.

The more you do this, the more the Prover will prove it so, and the Thinker will transform into a Knower. When you change your worldview, you change your experience of reality. The optimist and the pessimist are both powerful creators of reality. The only difference is that one moves toward manifesting the best out of situations while the other moves toward manifesting the worst. Which side do you want to be on?

Once you have reached the level of the Knower, you'll have an unshakeable conviction that gets you through the hardest of times. This is because the Knower always has faith. You'll no longer be wondering "if" your desires will manifest, but you'll *know* that it's only a matter of "when" they will come to fruition.

I'll end this chapter with a magnificent quote from Ram Dass that sums it all up.

> *"Everywhere you look, you see what you are looking for.*
> *When you are looking for God, all you see is God."*
> **—Ram Dass**

CHAPTER 7:

TAKING THE FAST LANE TO EVERYTHING YOU WANT

SECRET #7: LIVE FROM THE END

*"If you hear a voice within you say you cannot paint,
then by all means paint and that voice will be silenced."*
—Vincent Willem van Gogh

Vincent van Gogh left his mark on humanity. If we analyze his quote, there is wisdom in his words. The modern equivalent would be "Fake it till you make it." But what does that mean? It means imitating the characteristics of your desired future self (version 2.0) until it becomes a part of who you are now. It means embodying who you want to be until you get what you want.

Sometimes, this technique works wonders, especially if it helps you identify certain internal blocks you didn't realize you had. For example, faking confidence can help you manifest situations you didn't think possible. All it takes is a little bit of pretending. This doesn't work all the time, of course. Situations can arise that test the fragility of the technique—and you can lose focus and reveal the 'true you.' For example, if you have not dealt with certain emotions, external triggers might cause them to surface during your 'act,' revealing the person 'behind the mask.'

In other cases, this technique causes people to experience imposter syndrome—they doubt their abilities. They feel like frauds; like they do not deserve what they have. This is the fragile side of the "Fake it till you make it" technique. If you give in to the feeling, it can have counter-effects, causing you to feel unworthy, incapable, or like you are not enough.

Of course, experiencing imposter syndrome is not always a bad thing. Feeling like an imposter could also mean you've stepped into the unknown, the realm of uncertainty. This means you're growing, and that's a good thing. However, an even better approach to this is to use what I call the "Be it till you are it" technique. This method builds from the core of your being—instead of pretending, you are developing. Instead of making, you are becoming. When you do this, you drown out (in a sustainable, long-lasting way) doubts and limiting beliefs that hold you back. In the words of van Gogh, "Paint until the voice is silenced."

This is the foundation of what we'll explore in this chapter. We're going to use the neuroscientific Hebbian Principle of "What fires together, wires together" and discover how you can tap into the energy of your version 2.0. An example of this mechanism in practice would be the "What Would Buddha Do?" mantra modern-day Buddhists invoke when dealing with issues that challenge their moral codes. Of course, the Buddhist practitioner taps into the archetypal idea of Buddha and uses it as a Tulpa (a being or object created through the power of imagination) of sorts, to influence their decision-making and help them change their behavior according to their will.

Applying this method to the realm of manifesting, you'll ask, "What would my future-accomplished-self do in my current situation? How would they respond to the obstacles that stand between me and my desired reality?" We call this "living from the end." It's a powerful technique for mastering the art of accelerated manifesting.

THE FORMULA FOR ACCELERATED MANIFESTING

We'll begin with a popular concept taught by NLP practitioners and life coaches alike that helps us understand how tapping into the frequency of our version 2.0 works. We call this *future presence,* and it follows the *be-do-have* formula.

First, what does it mean to 'be'? 'Being' comes from your core. It's a deep sense of knowing. When you are being in a particular way, the heart and mind are in agreement with each other. Here is a quick example. If you are attempting to manifest a million-dollar income—*who would you need to be to achieve that? How would you feel about the work you do? What level of confidence would you have? How would you carry yourself? How would you deal with difficult situations? How would you speak to others? What would the quality of your thoughts and emotions be? Where would you focus your attention?*

What type of person would you need to be to sustain a million-dollar income? This was part of the Chapter 1 exercises. In this chapter, you'll be looking at principles and techniques you can follow to put that clarity to use and start "being" your version 2.0.

Once you have a clear picture of who you'd need to be to sustain a million-dollar reality, the next step would be to incorporate the "do" aspect of the *be-do-have* formula. 'Doing' results from you 'being'—the second step follows the first step. When you make the choice (mentally and emotionally) to be a certain type of person, you take actions that support this way of being. These actions can manifest as intuitive hunches, spontaneous insights, and more conviction, inspiration, and control over what you choose to do or not do. Once you've embodied your version 2.0, the actions that follow come effortlessly. You don't need to overthink; you'll be open to experimenting, receiving feedback, and improving and optimizing your approach to achieve your goals. This isn't because you're motivated or because you *need* to or *should* do something, it's because you *are* the person who will achieve that thing, and you'll do what's needed to make it so.

The doing aspect of the *be-do-have* formula is just like "What Would Buddha Do?" It's placing yourself in the role of your version 2.0 and acting according to the principles of that persona—or that Tulpa. Tulpa is a Theosophical term that describes a 'being' created through spiritual or mental intentions. These beings have their own sentience and wills independent from their creators. In some forms of mysticism, a practitioner can 'wear the Tulpa' which will imbue them with the powers of that Tulpa. Invoking the archetypal energies of Buddha through the mantra "What Would Buddha Do?" is like *Tulpamancy*. When you have a defined picture of *who you are in your desired future*, and then behave according to the image you created in your mind in the present moment; you are tapping into the energetic frequency of your desired *future self*.

Here's where it gets interesting. Earlier I mentioned the Hebbian Principle of "What fires together, wires together." Neuroscientist Donald O. Hebb observed that when neurons run a neural circuit in your brain, they form *neural networks*. When someone behaves in a certain way, their neurons wire together to form a neural network—which has a higher capacity for processing information. It's also the way the brain automates cerebral algorithms. Physical changes happen in your brain to accommodate the new behavior. It takes eighteen to 254 days of repeated action to create a basic neural network in the brain. Therefore, when you embody the behaviors of your future-self in the present, you are doing several things:

- Tapping into the energetic signature of your future-self (frequency).
- Rewiring the brain and installing 'future self habits and responses.'
- Altering your identity consciously to resonate with your desired future.

You are changing your brain today to *become* your future self. The two first steps of the *be-do-have* formula are in a constant loop, feeding each other to improve all layers of the person you are choosing to be. Can you see how powerful this technique is? When we mentally and emotionally *feel into* the state of our future selves, we respond differently to the world—and it responds differently back. When you engage your senses, you engage your attention. The more you focus and merge with your version 2.0, the more you become it. Do this enough and one day you'll wake up to find that you have everything you desired. You didn't have to do anything special except take *simple, obvious steps* toward your aim every day, until one day, everything manifests according to your will.

This is the basic premise of the *be-do-have* formula. If you're committed enough, this formula can change your life.

REDEFINING FAILURE

While the *be-do-have* formula seems simple on paper, you will "fail." You may think that one habit is easy to install, only to discover that it's harder than you imagined. Such setbacks can make embodying your version 2.0 feel near-impossible. Some people who try this and fail allow failure to influence their future actions because they see it as failure. They focus on *moving away from pain rather than moving toward desire.* If we see redirections as failures, we'll limit how much we learn from them.

What if failure didn't exist? It's true, we all make mistakes on our path. That's inevitable. However, a mistake doesn't have to be a failure…it can be an *opportunity* to gain understanding. Let's say, for example, that your version 2.0 reads a book a month to expand their knowledge in a particular field of interest. Perhaps you decide you too can exercise this simple habit—but every time you sit down to read, an external force steals your attention. After a month, you haven't finished a single book. You feel the sting of "failure." You feel you're "doing it wrong" and not manifesting.

What if, instead of feeling like a failure, you use this as an opportunity to understand *what went wrong?* Instead of wallowing in defeat, take a pen and paper, sit down, and reflect on your past activities. Perhaps you realize your original thought was ambitious, and that your schedule makes it hard to behave according to your plan. So, you adapt your behavior. You block out a few hours a week for reading and try again, or you re-set your milestone to read just a page a day. Mistakes and setbacks are not failures. They are opportunities to adjust your trajectory—every time you "fail", you learned a way of how *not* to do it.

We aren't all-knowing wizards who can predict our futures. We can work from the perspective of our desired future self, but cannot get it right 100 percent of the time. It's okay to have expectations, but make sure these don't become attachments. When you believe you've failed, it's because you are attached to an outcome. Not getting what you think you wanted causes pain and suffering. Rather than using an unexpected outcome to your advantage, you fall into a comparison trap that separates you from your desired future self.

Within the infinite mind of the Universe, there are many iterations of your desire. Since reality always takes the path of least resistance, your current perceived failure means only that there is a better way to do X, Y, or Z, and that what has manifested is the Universe's way of putting you on a simpler path. Whenever you run into a wall, take a step back. Observe what you did, and reflect on what you can learn from the experience.

Remember, reality will test your resolve, but always to manifest your desire in the *simplest way possible*. This sounds paradoxical, but it's how it works. Think, for example, about raising a child. For a while, you tie their shoes for them. At some point, you stop tying their shoes, and let them learn it for themselves. If you were to keep tying their shoes, they'd grow up and become an adult who can't tie their shoes. Being a person who never *learned how to learn* is a limited way to live. To be limitless is to embrace your limitless nature; to give yourself the chance to grow into a person who knows how to 'tie their shoes,' rather than wishing and hoping for the Universe to do it for you. This is how reality takes the most convenient path.

However, this most convenient path will not always fall within the boundaries of your current paradigm. Often, what manifests exists outside the parameters you envisioned. Remain unattached to outcomes. Then pivot and roll with the punches.

When we work on embodying our version 2.0, we are convinced that because we are not "good enough" now, our limits of today define our limits of tomorrow. But when was van Gogh *not* an artist? Did he ever feel the *need to become* an artist, or was he an artist before he picked up his first paintbrush? The answer? van Gogh was always an artist, even when he knew nothing about technique, color combinations, oil paint, and so forth. Before his paintings became popular, he was already the genius he always was. It just hadn't reflected in his physical environment yet.

Like van Gogh, you *already are* who you wish to become. It's a matter of embracing that side of you and allowing it to shine forth in your energy. If you weren't already who you wanted to be, you wouldn't even be able to think it up. *The only evidence we ever need to know that our version 2.0 is a real possibility is when we can envision and feel into it.*

Think about any skill you have learned over the years. Go back to the beginning of your journey. Were you a different *being* back then, or the same person who dedicated time and energy toward achieving that goal?

Your mind may have changed, your perspectives may have shifted, but you are always *you*. Right now, you are the 'past of your future self' while being the "future of your past self." It's all a matter of perspective. We're always becoming. By following this principle, we focus our energy on the act of becoming/creating rather than on expecting an outcome. This is a powerful truth that, if understood, will improve your ability to manifest.

REWRITING YOUR STORY

We've discussed future presence—tapping into the archetypal energy of our version 2.0. But how do we go about it? One way we can accelerate change in our lives is by *rewriting our personal narratives*. You may scratch your head and think, "My past is set in stone. How can I rewrite my narrative? Isn't that lying to myself?"

Everything you think about who you are—your past events and memories—is not 100 percent accurate. Sure, you can recall events, but as we talked about earlier in this book, every time you remember something, you alter its meaning. This is because when the brain stores a memory, certain neurons adjust their connections. When we recall these memories, we alter these connections as our current moods and expectations influence the nature of the memory. If you recall a memory enough times, you can alter your perception of events and re-envision what happened. This happens more frequently than we would like to admit. Depending on how we frame these stories, our memories could be as accurate as… well…a guess.

What this means is that we often have the tendency to fill our personal narratives with biases that can work against us. We have the power to alter our perspective of a memory—meaning we have the power to reframe our narratives. For example, let's say that when you were a child, someone made fun of how you spoke. This experience influenced your ability to speak up and express your opinion in public. However, as an adult, you now possess the understanding that the child who made fun of you back then had their own set of issues and didn't know any better. You can reframe the meaning behind their actions.

Many people who suffer early in life use their past as fuel to prove people wrong. While this perspective can be okay to generate that initial jolt of motivation for you to achieve your goals, it will never produce long-lasting results. A better way to frame an unpleasant memory is to use the moment of recollection to generate self-love and compassion without seeking external validation. There is a lot of power in loving yourself, regardless of what others tell you. Not to say that you should remain complacent, but you can seek to grow while still feeling like you are enough. Expect great things from yourself, because you deserve the best.

We can also choose to reframe our narratives by recalling a traumatic event. Many people, when recalling such moments, assume they are the cause for their current lack and struggle. This could be the case, especially if the event altered your mental and emotional state. However, I like to live by the saying "there is always a way." Even if you can't see it yet, it's there. We start by changing the meaning we place on a traumatic event. *When we change what a past event means to us, we change the effect it has on us.*

Remember, we get to choose what we do with our suffering. As Alan Watts once put it,

> *"There will always be suffering.*
> *But we must not suffer over the suffering."*

You can recall a memory and become mindful of it, observing the memory as if it were a movie, separate from self. Using your current understanding of life, you then rationalize and ascribe new meaning to the events or let go of the energetic attachment to the memory itself—altering your past narrative.

Finally, as far-fetched as this may sound, you can frame your future projections as a memory. If you've taken the time to meditate on, visualize, and feel into the experiences of your version 2.0, you can use this as a past reference point to define who you are today. Remember, the only moment in time that exists is now, therefore, any alteration to your "past" or "future" is valid. Isn't this fascinating? Of course, this isn't something you want to tell people who know you, as you can't "prove" it. Only you can experience that moment. For this to work, only you need to believe it to be true. You don't want to be lying about credentials you haven't yet achieved, either. The point of this exercise is to reference more often the energy of your version 2.0 so you can experience being in and embodying that state—that should be your focal point.

Now, how do we know which memories we need to let go of and work on? Whenever you feel anxious, stressed, angry, fearful, etc., instead of giving in to the emotion, take a moment. Step back. Take a few breaths. Gauge how strong the feeling is by assigning it a value between one and ten. Ask yourself, *"When was the last time I felt like this?"* Allow your mind to give you an image or feeling. Once you have identified the previous similar instance, examine that memory. Become mindful of it. Once you have understood the conditions that made you feel like that, ask, *"When was the first time I felt like this?"* Wait. Try to recall the "starting point" of this emotion. What event caused it? What perspective do you have of this event? How has this framed your perspective of yourself and your reality?

If you do this correctly, your mind will prompt a memory attached to the feeling. Within this memory, you can implement the editing technique, reassigning meaning or letting go of your attachment to it.

Sometimes you need to forgive the person who offended you. At other times, you need to provide comfort to the image of you in that memory. But by trusting your creative unconscious, you can rewrite your personal narrative, release yourself from the bondage of the past, and recreate it into something that benefits you and lifts you up. It's not always easy or pleasurable—but for those brave enough to venture into the past, it's a powerful way to accelerate internal change.

Now let's look at ways of using this newly defined personal narrative so we can turn this into a practice we can implement daily. But before we do, let's look at what I like to call "the sweet spot" of manifesting.

THE BALANCE BETWEEN INTENTION AND SURRENDER

By now you have realized that accelerated manifesting requires the clarity of knowing what you want and the ability to allow yourself to receive it. This is what we call the balance between intention and surrender. Unless you are clear about your direction, you can never manifest in the way you intend. You need to have an initial intention and clarity around it—but you also need to trust the Universe in how it delivers it to you.

Because of our limited perceptions of reality, we do not know what the best outcome will be. We romanticize our desires, believing that only by taking a particular path will we achieve an optimal outcome. But when we allow reality to take the shape it must, we realize that we're allowing the manifestation of the desire to be *better* than what we expected or asked for. You may not intellectually know this…but the Universe does.

As we've discussed, if you trust that you are doing your part to manifest your true heart's desire, you don't have to worry about how the outcome comes to fruition—you only have to act in the present moment according to what you can do now to move toward that desire. Making space for your manifestations to unfold is crucial.

Often, to speed up the manifestation of what they want, people work harder than they need to. But by working harder, they spend unnecessary energy, leading to physical exhaustion, mental fatigue, stress, overwhelm, or frustration. They're out of alignment with the future self that *has* what they want.

Think about it. Does your future self feel the need to work hard to continue to have what they already have? They don't. Why? Because what they have is *normal* for them. The thing has already happened. It's already manifested. It's *known*.

In Chapter 3, we discussed Occam's Razor—when we take the simplest next step, we eliminate the resistance that can come with taking action (e.g., overthinking, doubting, supposed complexity, etc.), while making forward progress toward our goals. So, balance between intention and surrender is the fast lane of all manifestations—it's the perfect mix of creating and allowing. If you can grasp this truth, you will remove a lot of stress from your life.

FORWARD MOMENTUM

When we think about the term "acceleration," a lot of ideas, analogies, and concepts come to mind. One is *momentum*. We define momentum as the motion of a moving body measured by the product of its mass and velocity. If there is no motion, there is no momentum. If you've ever taken level one Physics, you might have heard of the snowball rolling down the hill analogy. As the snowball rolls down the hill, it grows larger and larger, gaining more mass, and as a result, momentum.

In accelerated manifesting, we aim to have momentum. It allows us to build consistency with our daily practices and keeps us focused even when we're faced with distractions or challenges. While everything we've discussed so far can help you build momentum, there are other approaches for creating momentum, too. One simple way is to know how to handle uninvited thoughts, emotions, and circumstances.

Technique #1: Good Morning Momentum

As we discussed earlier, we live in a world filled with distractions. There will always be a new trend, viral video, social event, TV series, etc. ready to scoop up our time and attention. The key is to catch yourself when these show up. When we're able to refocus our attention in these moments, we flip a switch in our internal algorithm, and we teach the brain to refocus whenever an external force steals our attention. But the question remains … *How do we do this?* One way is to start positive momentum in the morning.

When we go to sleep, we reset ourselves energetically. When you're in a sleeping state, you're neither happy nor sad. You're neutral. Upon waking, how you choose to spend your morning is how you kick-start your momentum. Taking up activities such as meditation, yoga, or journaling are excellent ways to kick-start your energy in the right direction. Other activities (such as getting into a fight with your partner, rushing to get to work, or giving into road rage) will have the opposite effect.

Technique #2: Conscious Choices

Another way of maintaining positive momentum is by making *conscious choices*. This means that every time you are about to engage in some sort of activity or task, step back. Make the *choice* to engage with it. Most people don't realize that they don't always choose their actions consciously. Their conditioning and old neural programs make their choices for them—they act unconsciously. Being mindful of the simplest choices you make teaches you to live a conscious life, led by your intent (as opposed to your urges). When we develop this skill, our focus skyrockets, because nothing 'out there' can ever influence where you place your attention.

On top of the constant propaganda we're bombarded with daily, we also have *internal forces* to deal with. When we feel positive or negative emotions or think positive or negative thoughts, we make choices about what to do with them. To illustrate, let's start with the negative ones. When some people feel a negative emotion or think a negative thought, their natural reaction is to resist. They place labels and point fingers. They fight. They question their own abilities. But the worst thing you can do in these situations is to judge yourself. Remember, it's normal to experience negativity, and it doesn't mean you're not on the right path. It means there are energies that need to be worked through. Let go. Allow them to run their course until you are back in a neutral state. Then redirect the leftover energy into a thought or object of focus that is more beneficial to you. The Center your Awareness exercise in Chapter 2 can certainly help with this.

Technique #3: Allowing the Shift

Whenever you experience a negative thought or emotion, it's best to be like an Aikido master. Aikido is an ancient martial arts form that takes a variety of different styles. What's interesting about Aikido is that it's a non-competitive sport, meaning there is no winner or loser. Unlike other self-defense martial arts practices, the goal of Aikido is to defend yourself while not hurting the attacker.

We can translate Aikido to "the way of the harmonious spirit." To use life energy (both negative and positive) to your benefit is the Aikido way. *This* is how you transform your inner critic into your inner fan. It's never by forcing the 'attacker' to do what you want or fighting them. The attacker in this case can represent the ego or negative thoughts, emotions, circumstances, people, etc. The goal is to use their 'weight' to your benefit to flip the situation.

You can't avoid conflict, but you can learn to use it to pivot and redirect. Roadblocks are nothing more than railroad switches. The process is never to jump from a negative state to a positive one. It's jumping from a negative state to a neutral one, *then* to a positive one. Think back, for example, to a time when you argued with a friend and then resolved it with a smile. In such circumstances, rarely do you jump from a heated discussion to uncontrollable laughter. The humor starts when you've changed the subject to something else first. That said, it's important to read every situation for what it is. Sometimes, a roadblock or an obstacle is reality telling you to slow down and rest. Remember, recovery is also forward movement. At other times, it's beneficial to plow ahead and take massive action. Be mindful of which is the best approach at any moment in time.

When momentum has kick-started and life happens fast, unique challenges can arise. For example, we can feel overwhelmed or anxious, and emotions—both negative and positive—can run high. The choice you make at these times is crucial, both for dealing with challenges and for getting the most out of them. We've discussed in this chapter how to rewrite your personal story and how to maintain momentum. Now it's time to see how we can manage it all at once and *increase momentum* when faced with unique challenges. Let's look at two practical ways of doing this.

OVERCOMING OVERWHELM

On this path of accelerated manifesting, you may find yourself overwhelmed, especially when attempting things outside of your comfort zone. But we can use moments of overwhelm as opportunities to maintain—or even gain—momentum. When you feel anxious about a situation or action, your nervous system is on alert. Every time you feel fear or anxiety, the sympathetic nervous system gets activated—which makes you pay attention to your immediate environment. This heightened state of awareness provides an opportunity for you to shift your internal programming and cerebral algorithms. You do this by reframing your feelings of supposed fear and nervousness and transforming them into *excitement*.

According to research conducted at Harvard Business School, you can increase your performance by *reappraising your anxiety for excitement*. When people are nervous, they try to "calm down," yet according to research by Harvard Business School professor Dr. Alison Wood Brooks, it takes less effort to reframe anxiety as excitement. Neurologically, the latter emotion is closer to anxiety than calmness. Thus, when you do something outside your comfort zone, and you feel a shiver of anxiety cloud your judgment, take a few breaths. Reframing your anxiety as excitement can increase the odds of success. For example, by saying "I'm excited!" or "Get excited!" out loud, study participants shifted their mindset to an optimistic, resourceful state, and looked forward to the experience (as opposed to fearing it every step of the way). It's surrendering to the moment and using fear as an indicator that you're on a fresh path that might benefit you.

Of course, reframing your anxiety as excitement takes time—but the next time you feel overwhelmed with anxiety, say, "I'm excited about what I'm about to do," and then dive in. Two things can happen: either you make it work, or you don't. However, priming your mind to interpret anxiety as excitement will enable you to take chances you wouldn't otherwise take. Every time you succeed in whatever task you are doing—it will create a feedback loop that will continue to build on your momentum for more efficient and accelerated manifesting.

HYPER-LEARNING

Stepping into the unknown can bring many blessings, but also a plethora of heightened emotions—fear, excitement, embarrassment, nervousness, joy—all of which keep your body alert. Your brain becomes receptive and your entire being becomes present. *You pay attention.*

The moment you experience intense negative and positive emotions can be an excellent time to hyper-learn. Hyper-learning is the ability to learn mentally, emotionally, and behaviorally at a sped-up rate, using the highest levels of human cognitive and emotional performance. By utilizing intense emotion to your benefit, not only do you allow the emotion to run its course, you ingrain new information in your brain.

Post-Traumatic Stress Disorder (PTSD) is a negative form of hyper-learning. The moment a traumatic event happens, and emotions are elevated, the brain learns from the experience, tucking it away into the unconscious layers of the mind and body. In a positive form of hyper-learning, the only difference is that you *choose what you want to learn*. Many people would rather suppress and/or repress negative emotions so they can stop feeling them. They're afraid of the discomfort or effect it will bring them and others. With accelerated manifesting, this can be counterproductive.

The goal is to use these moments to build *positive* momentum. So, next time you feel an intense negative emotion, ask yourself, "What do I want to learn at this moment?" You can learn about a new way of seeing a particular event or a new way of performing a particular action. This is how you make the most of your mistakes. For building positive momentum with positive emotions such as joy, confidence, or excess vitality, try using the Bagha technique to anchor that emotional state and use it as fuel. The Bagha technique is an ancient method of signaling to the brain to "pay attention." Place the tip of your tongue on the roof of your mouth and then make a power statement in your mind. For example, when you finish a lot of work and feel satisfied about your efforts, do the Bagha technique. Say something like, "I can complete great works!" This process imprints the experience into your consciousness and keeps your mind focused, which empowers you to achieve any desire you have. This is another form of amplifying the benefits of positive emotions.

Many people get lost in emotion during peak events in their

lives. However, if you stay conscious in these moments, you have the opportunity for significant personal transformation.

ACTION AND REFLECTION

I dedicated this chapter to tapping into your resourceful future self and bringing that energy into your reality. You may invoke your future self in your daily life, but you need to be engaged with the present in order to 'steer the ship.' Being mindful and reflecting on the happenings of your day allows you to read each moment so you know when to pivot and when to stop and rest. It's making the best of your reality; using *what is* to your advantage.

By mastering the techniques discussed in this chapter, you will experience an accelerated life. You'll notice that the more you let go of control and surrender to the flow of the Universe while taking forward strides to manifest your intentions, the easier things get. Once you grasp the power of living from the end, the end you once dreamed about becomes your beginning.

Final Thoughts

Throughout this book, we have taken a layered approach to accelerating your ability to manifest. By now, you have realized that many of these principles, exercises, and techniques are about taking action; about moving forward with your intentions and giving them room to come to fruition. The Universe is always open to giving you your heart's genuine desire, but if you'd like to speed up the process, meet it halfway. Know how to navigate the inevitable tests that will come. This is the fundamental Law of Attraction principle that many people get wrong. You don't simply ask for what you want and wait until it delivers. You state your mission—your intent—and *move toward it like there is no other direction you'd rather go.*

It's when you commit to this process that you see the magic of the Universe unfold. Have faith in the process and develop conviction in your actions. Pull your desired future reality into the present moment, in every way—for that is the key to supercharging your reality. This is when things happen out of the blue and the cosmos conspires in your favor. You cannot pursue your deepest desires half-heartedly. You must be enveloped in the reality of their existence, make decisions with conviction, and know that it will manifest, somehow in some way.

Accelerated manifesting is about learning how to maintain focus while surrendering to the flow. The first step is to gain clarity around your intentions and let go of your attachments. Understand that who you *think* you are, is often standing in the way of who you *could be*. Realize that action always trumps inaction. When you run out of options, there are ways to shake the snowball to generate new thoughts, emotions, and insights. Often, this comes by taking the simplest, most obvious next step toward your goals.

Understand that you'll be uncomfortable at certain moments in your life—and that's okay. Outside your comfort zone is a realm of discomfort—and beyond that lies everything you ever wanted. The more we expand our comfort zone, the more comfortable we become with all aspects of reality, giving us the ability to manage our energy and make conscious choices that lead to better results. It is when you let go of your attachment to comfort, and release your resistance to discomfort, that you fall in tandem with the flow of the Universe.

By finding what is beautiful in your life and training your mind to notice it, appreciate it, and amplify it, you'll fuel your belief system with everything you need to kick-start momentum and put you on the fast lane to getting what you want.

Is it that easy? Not always, but it is simple. It can get easier the more you practice these principles. The point of this book has been not only to give you the theory, but also to provide practical examples on how you too can shift your state to live a more accelerated, magnetic life. Armed with this knowledge, I encourage you to practice incorporating these teachings into your daily life. Some will mesh with your personality. Others will be more difficult, so take your time. Test them out. Find out which ones resonate with you the most.

All the practices in this book will speed up your ability to manifest. When we stretch the confines of our perceived reality and identity, we access new levels of wisdom that we otherwise would be unreceptive to. Stepping beyond what you know while maintaining consistent alignment with your crystal clear vision is the goal.

Now that you have a toolbox filled with timeless principles and practical exercises to accelerate your manifesting journey, one question remains: *What are you going to do with it?*

A Short Message From The Author

Hey there, did you enjoy the book? Hopefully you did! A lot of work, research, and collaborations took place to make this book what it is today. So, if you enjoyed *Accelerated Manifesting*, I'd love to hear your thoughts in the review section on Amazon.com. It helps me gain valuable feedback to produce the highest quality content for all of my beautiful readers. Even just a short 1-2 sentence review would mean the WORLD to me.

>> Scan the QR Code above
to leave a short review on Amazon <<

Thank you from the bottom of my heart for purchasing and reading it to end.

Sincerely,

Ryuu

References

Brittanica. (n.d.). Sunyata. In *Encyclopædia Brittanica.* Retrieved December 3, 2021, from https://www.britannica.com/topic/sunyata

Brooks, A. W. (2014). Get excited: Reappraising pre-performance anxiety as excitement. *Journal of Experimental Psychology: General, 143*(3), 1144-1158. https://doi.org/10.1037/a0035325

Lewis, R. (2013, September 26). *Purpose-Driven Life – A Psychiatrist's Evolutionary Perspective on Human Motivation.* James Randi Educational Foundation. http://archive.randi.org/site/index.php/swift-blog/2223-purpose-driven-life-a-psychiatrists-evolutionary-perspective-on-human-motivation.html

MMC Inc. (n.d.). *Sudden Wealth Sydrome.* http://www.mmcinstitute.com/about-2/sudden-wealth-syndrome/

NEFE. (2018, January 12). *Research Statistic on Financial Windfalls and Bankruptcy.*

https://www.nefe.org/news/2018/01/research-statistic-on-financial-windfalls-and-bankruptcy.aspx

Zeland, V. (2011). *Reality transurfing.* Winchester: John Hunt Publishing.

Made in United States
North Haven, CT
24 February 2023

33126577R00089